GOOD
PARTIES

LEE BAILEY'S
GOOD
PARTIES

Favorite Food, Tableware, Kitchen Equipment, and More, to Make Entertaining a Breeze

Text and Photographs
by Lee Bailey

Clarkson N. Potter, Inc./Publishers
DISTRIBUTED BY CROWN PUBLISHERS, INC., NEW YORK

Special Acknowledgment

To the late Gloria Safier, my friend for almost thirty years and my agent for these last five. You left too soon. But thanks for all those wonderful memories I have because of you.

And thanks to my friends at Clarkson N. Potter who always do what they do so very well. And for all the others who were helpful in getting this project done.

Designed by Rochell Udell
and Douglas Turshen

Introduction, Menus, and Recipes
copyright © 1986 by Lee Bailey

Photographs copyright © 1986 by Lee Bailey

The four photographs appearing on pages 2–3, 46–47, 58–59, and 134–135 by Joshua Greene originally photographed for Australian *Vogue*. Copyright © 1986 by Joshua Greene. All rights reserved. Used by permission of the photographer.

Published by Clarkson N. Potter, Inc., 225 Park Avenue South, New York, New York 10003 and represented in Canada by the Canadian MANDA Group
CLARKSON N. POTTER, POTTER, and colophon are trademarks of Clarkson N. Potter, Inc.

Manufactured in Japan

Library of Congress Cataloging-in-Publication Data
Bailey, Lee.
  Good parties.
  Includes index.
  1. Entertaining. 2. Menus. I. Title.
TX731.B3 1986   642   86–77
ISBN 0-517-55934-X
10 9 8 7 6 5 4 3 2 1

First Edition

Whenever I give a party I think is really good,
I know it is that way in part because of a secret
ingredient I have—
my friends. So this book is for them.

Contents

Introduction

Good parties are, at least partially, a frame of mind. Start with the assumption that the whole point is for you and company to enjoy yourselves. An obvious goal, but, from what I have seen and experienced, one that can easily get muddled and lost to overreaching, poor planning, and wrong choices. So get your priorities right and pay attention to details—everything else will follow.

Begin by asking yourself if your party plan will make your job as hostess easier and pleasant and your guests comfortable. If the answer is negative, you had better get back to the drawing board. And while you are analyzing, ask yourself what kind of party suits you. For some it is the big, swirling buffet. For others it is the cocktail party or a formal dinner. For me, since I want to talk to people and hear what they have to say, it is the small dinner party for six to eight. However, it really doesn't matter which you prefer; just do what you like. And your guests will probably be happy too.

Now before we get down to the nuts and bolts of planning, a word about guests. As I said in my dedication, my secret weapon is my friends—a pretty outgoing and talkative bunch. Such people help make an evening "go" and are a good nucleus. While I seem to have more than my share of these types in my life, in truth it takes only a single good talker to keep things rolling. If one is not included in your gathering, then you have to take on the role. And while we are at it, there are some people who just like to listen. Let them be observers if they seem more comfortable that way.

Many things you may not have thought of can contribute to a good party—for instance, the shape of the dining table. For my money, you just can't beat a round one. It democratically brings everyone together in such a way as to allow each guest to see the others, making them all an equal part of the group—encouraging general conversation rather than the more limited "right to left, left to right" option you have seated at a rectangle. In this day and age of limited space, where the "dining room" is frequently not a room at all, but part of a larger open area, round tables often relate to their surroundings in a more aesthetically pleasing way. And speaking of space, you can certainly squeeze in a greater number at a round table than a rectangle would accommodate. As a matter of fact, you can keep adding guests until there is no knee room left. Sometimes this crowding is even a bit of a plus, creating a kind of festive camaraderie. I realize I'm putting a lot of emphasis on the joys and advantages of a round table, but I don't mean to imply that if you don't have one all is lost. Remember, all things are relative, and many, many more than the shape of the table go into the making of an evening.

But while we are on the subject of the furniture, let me add that I like my dining chairs to have some back support. However, I don't think they all must have arms. And certainly, when space is limited, side (armless) chairs take less room. For larger groups, you can supplement your dining chairs with folding ones stashed in the closet—comfort and support are the rule here as well.

About lighting, an element that has not, until fairly recently, been given as much attention as it should: A bright overhead light in the dining room can be pretty brutal, and people are never more aware of this than when they are trapped under one. Let's face it, we are all vain enough to want to look our best, especially if we are being observed at close quarters (as happens across a dining table), so see that the light is flattering.

The best solution is to start with a source of general light that can be regulated. A dimmer added to the switch is a very worthwhile investment indeed. When the overall light is balanced, accent with pools of brighter, but soft, light. Of course, candles are the easiest choice here. And speaking of lighting intensity, I remember someone telling me an interesting story about a problem encountered when the vast Radio City Music Hall opened in New York City. Its scale and Deco decorations were the talk of the town—so much talk, in fact, that the excited conversation in the foyer regularly carried over into the auditorium where the picture was being shown, disturbing the patrons watching the movie. A lighting consultant was called in, and his solution was to dim all the lights in the large public areas, which had been brightly lit to better reveal the wondrous new space with its modern design and murals. This clever fellow had observed that people tend to quiet down as the lights are lowered—even to whisper. That is why, to this day, the wattage is so meager that you practically trip over the furniture in the theater's lounges.

You might use this little piece of knowledge yourself. If you put together a group of guests who don't know one another very well, turn all the lights up while the group is getting acquainted over cocktails. Bright lights make people more talkative. Then turn the lights down somewhat after the party gets under way. This works; I've tried it.

So long as we are on cocktails, maybe this is a good place to tell you what I think of extensive hors d'oeuvres. Quite candidly: not much. I've never been able to see the logic in having dinner before you have dinner—which these endless and sumptuous hors d'oeuvres before dining amount to. If you have spent time and effort on a meal, why blunt everyone's appetite beforehand? Keep it light.

Another thought: We tend to get used to things being a certain way and often ignore the pleasure of change. Say you are having a spring lunch and there happens to be a part of your garden in spectacular bloom, which can be seen to best advantage from a window in the living room. Why not move, or set up, a table there for the meal? However, resist making changes for their own sake, just to be doing something.

OK, so you don't want to move the furniture; then rearrange the guests. I do. For instance, I have a very large round table in the country. It seats eight comfortably and ten or more noisily. But when I have only four or five people, I don't spread them evenly around the table. Instead, I seat them in a crescent to one side, which makes the focus the opposite side of the table, where I have placed the flowers. You might do the same. Or if yours is a big rectangular table with only a few guests, try grouping everyone together at one end, the way it is sometimes done in French country restaurants. This creates a very intimate and convivial atmosphere.

Back to flowers for a minute: I am partial to small, low bouquets in multiples. This solution seems much more desirable to me than having one imposing "arrangement" plunked dead center, flanked by tall tapers. When I see such a combination, I know I'm in for a serious evening. Leave that to your mother-in-law.

On the question of music: I really enjoy it, but it can be in conflict at a party. Are we to listen or talk to one another? Music loud enough to actually be appreciated can make conversation difficult. On the other hand, having no music is almost preferable to "elevator music." Whatever kind you choose, do the choosing in advance and be set up so you will have one less thing to concern yourself with during the evening.

Another important something that you should do to make your parties run with ease is realize that as hostess you are the director of the occasion. For example, it is up to you to tell your guests where you would like them to sit when you gather at the table. You should also take the lead, showing by your example, in how the meal is to be served. If you feel more comfortable serving all the plates in the kitchen before placing them, then get the guests seated and go to it. Handling the service this way means you won't necessarily need any sort of serving table or buffet. However, if you like to put everything out on a sideboard or serving cart and let guests serve themselves (with your guidance), plan accordingly to make it run. Still another way is to put the main course in front of your place at the table and serve it from there, enlisting a guest to add the accompaniments as plates are passed around. This is how I do it. One advantage to my method is that it, too, requires no serving table.

For those evenings when I have a large group, I let the dining table act as the buffet. Of course, an extra table standing nearby does come in handy, and can save steps—a convenient spot to put coffee and dessert things to wait until they are needed. (Make it a folding cart that can be stored when not in use if space is tight.)

Anyway, the choice is yours, when you know how you like to do things. In truth, any variation is fine so long as it works. The important thing is to know what you plan to do.

All the general rules and cautions still apply in more uncommon situations. That is, the occasion must be thought out and *you* and your guests must be made comfortable—as when your setup does not include a permanent dining area, for instance. This presents an unusual set of problems, which may be solved in the usu-al manner. Since in this case you will not be eating under the most ideal conditions, devise a menu that includes food which is easy to eat. No sauces, nothing messy, and nothing that will require too much cutting. Bread, if you are having it, should be prebuttered, and salad should be chopped. And since you will probably have to press an odd piece of furniture such as an end table or chest into service to serve from, be sure it is convenient. Coffee tables are not the best solution for this, because they usually are too low. Also be sure you know where you will want everyone to sit when there is no dining table—and tell them. Don't just leave this to chance.

The same kind of easy-to-eat food would do for a picnic if you live within reasonable distance of a park or open wooded area. Let the leafy outdoors be your dining room. Or simply employ the picnic idea indoors and spread a blanket on your apartment floor. In short, use your imagination and tailor the meal to fit the circumstance.

Finally, what almost all these simple observations and advice rest on is (once again) careful planning and analysis of your needs—reflecting your own style and way of doing things. The style itself is up to you. And so far as I am concerned, the more personal (or idiosyncratic), the better. What counts is *knowing* your own style well enough to make things flow seamlessly.

Since I am basically a designer, I thought that this time around it might be fun, as well as useful, to show what that aspect of my interests is all about. So in addition to suggesting food and showing ways to serve it, the book is meant to be an example and a source book, too.

Along the way you will see a sampling of my favorite dinnerware, flatware, glassware, and table linen. And, included for their design and function both, an assortment of cooking utensils and cooking and entertaining miscellany—and gadgets. (I must confess to a great weakness for gadgets.)

My interest in the design of things—almost everything—has been with me for as long as I can recall. And I found, after studying design and later on teaching it, what pleasure there is in encouraging and helping those who share this interest. This has led me to believe that more people than is generally imagined have talent, which is often revealed by the very freedom to explore. Should any proof be needed on that score, all you have to do is look in on a kindergarten and watch the children unselfconsciously expressing themselves, sometimes in startlingly original ways. At some point this natural ability and curiosity (which can bring great satisfaction) seem to be thwarted in many of us, making us begin to doubt our power to make design choices for ourselves. The truth is, we all know more than we think we do. Ultimately it is the expression of this unique self that gives any design project its distinction. While some have more of a knack for this than others, almost anyone who has enough general enthusiasm for the subject to want to explore it in the first place can begin to choose, with just a little direction and encouragement.

On the following pages you will find a very narrow and personal point of view. The reasoning behind such a limited focus is to more clearly show the foundation on which my decisions are built. Hopefully, my example will provide some useful insights and a key to the basic selection process. In order to make your own choices you must become aware of and use that germ of consistency lurking in whatever you do and do not like.

I have noticed that a large part of the population have plenty to say about what they don't like (about everything), but comparatively little about the opposite. I believe this is so not only because of some vague insecurity about having their taste judged, but because being negative is plain easier. The positive path—in design, at least—is to strive to define what pleases you and why.

I also want to say that you should not conclude that because a particular item or group of items happens not to be included here I feel it or they have no value. It is entirely possible to see the design sound-ness in an object and still not want to own it. For instance, you won't see much majolica in the book, because it never has appealed to me very strongly, and the same with Art Deco—although both are currently enjoying a great popularity. This is solely a matter of personal taste. But more important, in this case, if my example is to be revealing or instructive, it must be limited. Hopefully, what is lost to omission will be more than compensated for in clarity.

Now about the food itself. Included are many dishes that I have come to enjoy over the years, some old, some new. They are typically easy to prepare, and still have that familiar down-home quality that will always be there in my food. These meals are a reflection of what I like right now, which hasn't changed much since I first started cooking, except that it seems to have become freer as it has been expanded to include dishes and ingredients I have come across along the way.

The book is divided into country and city sections, because I divide my time between the two places. And, as was the case with the previous books, I give a general game plan to help guard against the occasion's becoming frazzling instead of fun.

I'd also like to say that these meals do not have to be literally re-created to be successful. Although there are times when two dishes are meant to complement each other, there are plenty of places where substitutions may be made, expecially in the kinds of vegetables you serve with the main course. Once you understand the essence of a menu, you should feel quite comfortable using other vegetables (as well as other accompaniments) that are your favorites or perhaps are more readily available than the ones suggested. The same might be said for some of the ingredients in the recipes themselves, although this may be trickier.

And, although I have said it before, it might be worth repeating that as nice as it is to have breads and biscuits with a meal, they are one of the first things you might leave out. As for desserts, so much is available ready-made these days that you may not want to bother making them. All of this is just another way of saying trust your own tastes and instincts. If you make a few mistakes, you will only be like the rest of us.

Since most people give large parties infrequently, almost all the recipes that follow serve six. This seems about the average number you find at dinner parties. And recipes for six can usually be stretched to accommodate eight without too much risk of foul-up. For bigger gatherings, many of these recipes may be doubled, but I find that, with the possible exceptions of sauces, soups, and stews, it is always better to make two batches of a dish than to try to make one double.

So give it some thought and celebrate—whatever—by giving a smashing little party.

—LEE BAILEY
New York City

GOOD
PARTIES

THE SUMMER HOUSE

The Summer House

With the dawning of the first changeable days of April, it's back to the country house on the weekends for me. My time during these beginning weeks is almost entirely taken up with raking, cleaning, and planting the garden. A race with the calendar always develops trying to get all this done, but it is a task I love. My degree of grousing and harrumphing would let anyone know immediately how much I like it. Common and sure symptoms. On Saturday nights, when my friends and I gather at one of our houses, the theme that introduces the evening always centers on how hard it is to get anyone to give you a helping hand and how unreliable any such help is, even when promised—and how bad the traffic in the village has become, and how deplorable all the new houses are that have sprung up since last fall. Any half-aware observer would quickly pick up on how pleased we are to be out there after a winter holed up in the city. We are back to our predictable pleasures. Food I choose now is usually hardy—something that can simmer unattended. These meals are characteristically nourishing not only for the body but also for the soul, tending to be composed mostly of old standbys (what I call "reward food"). It is about now, too, when I will try to get in at least one good oyster fry, while oysters are still big and fat, before they get slimmed down for the summer. This meal is one I am especially fond of. And if I have had the good luck to lay my hands on a bottle of homemade catsup (mine or someone else's) to accompany them, I really am in bliss.

Should the weather turn uncooperative (which you can depend on its doing), I'll go in for a little "serious" cooking. This helps keep me from being too disappointed that I can't get out there and scratch around in the yard. Also, there is something reliably pleasing about baking when it's threatening outside. Maybe it has to do with how inviting the oven makes the house smell. It is then that I'll gladly volunteer to make dessert for a friend—or surprise one of them.

As spring and summer progress and I get the out-of-doors under control, my thoughts turn to experimenting in the kitchen and having weekend guests. As I said before, food is never the sole focus of the weekend, but just one element, whose function is to make the whole occasion happy and relaxing. Meals always are shaped by what I see at the farm stands and how much time I have to allot to preparation.

I've noticed that my enthusiasm for certain dishes peaks and then wanes over a few years, so I never discard any special equipment I might have invested in just because I don't seem to use it much anymore. Sure enough, in a few summers the cycle will begin all over again, and I will renew my love affair with whatever had been out of favor for a while.

August is tomato month around here. It is also about the only month of the year when I consciously plan meals that might be considered light or "cooling." (I suspect these terms are questionable in most cases anyway, being in many ways more psychological than real.) Obviously, this is because by August we are in deep summer and everyone wants the living to be easy. Up until then I cook almost anything that I might want, regardless of whether it is considered a summer or winter dish. This is in part due to the fact that the weather remains cool in the evenings on the water—cool enough for a fire by nightfall—right up to the end of July. I have a real keenness for seafood salads and poached fish, both of which can be a bit time-consuming to do, so I save them for special lunches now. It also seems a good time to do seafood risotto. And an even better time for homemade ice cream!

So far as availability of produce is concerned, the fall is an absolute feast for the senses. Beginning in September and continuing on until the frost knocks out the tenderer plants, farm stands are bursting with marvelous dewy vegetables and fruit, everything from tiny dark eggplants to champagne grapes. After these come the fall and winter squash, pumpkins, and strong-flavored vegetables such as Brussels sprouts to take you into winter. Potatoes have been dug, among them my favorite, called "Green Mountain," which are perfect for mashing. And, of course, apples of every kind come tumbling out of baskets. A bonus from them is how wonderful they make the air smell indoors. I always buy more than I can use, finally winding up having to give them away, just because I can't resist their fresh, sweet odor. And with apples arrives apple cider, good not only for drinking but for cooking fresh ham. Add to this crystal-clear days and the harvest moon—is it any wonder that I am so crotchety for a time when I must go back to the city?

*Ham steak with pear sauce
and cheese spoon bread*

Country Ham Dinner

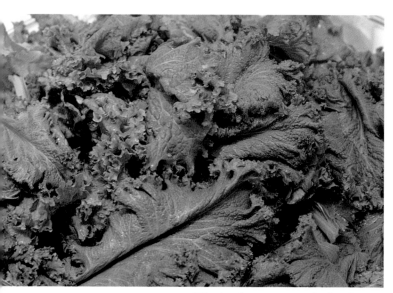

Mustard greens ready for the pot

Many hosts and hostesses seem to shy away from serving guests foods that are known as an acquired taste. I don't hold with that point of view, and think it is perfectly acceptable to serve a dish or two that one doesn't ordinarily have at a dinner party—although I don't think the meal should be composed entirely of "exotic" ingredients and dishes.

Anyway, you can see where I am heading—in this case it is mustard greens, a vegetable very popular in the South, as are all greens, with the possible exception of spinach. I love their flavor, and when I include mustard greens in a dinner menu more people like them than not. For those who don't, there is plenty else to eat, so they won't starve; while the others have had a little adventure. Personally, I am always delighted to find I like something that I had assumed I wouldn't.

To go with the mustard greens there are baked marinated ham steaks with pear sauce and cheese spoon bread. The dessert, mint julep ice cream, is the best use of bourbon I know of.

Baked Marinated Ham Steaks
Pear Sauce
Mustard Greens
Cheese Spoon Bread
Mint Julep Ice Cream
Wine
Coffee

Above: *Pear sauce surrounded by the ingredients for making it*
Left: *Mint Julep ice cream*

BAKED MARINATED HAM STEAKS

Not only are these no trouble to prepare and wonderfully flavorful and moist, baked ham steaks solve the dilemma of what to do with all that leftover meat baking a whole or half ham leaves you with.

Two 1-inch-thick ham slices, with bone left in (approximately 3½ pounds)
½ cup port or liquid from the Pear Sauce, below
½ cup safflower oil
¼ cup water
1 large garlic clove, crushed
2 bay leaves
6 drops Tabasco sauce
½ teaspoon salt
1 tablespoon fresh lemon juice
¼ teaspoon black pepper
4 tablespoons Worcestershire sauce
2 tablespoons tomato paste

Put the ham slices in a single layer in a Pyrex dish. Combine the remaining ingredients in a medium saucepan. Bring the mixture to a boil, then turn off the heat and let cool. Pour it over the ham and refrigerate, covered, overnight.

The next day, let the steaks return to room temperature in the marinade. Preheat the oven to 375 degrees.

Bake in the marinade for 45 minutes to 1 hour. Turn the steaks once during the cooking. Cut into serving portions.

Serves 6

PEAR SAUCE

Pear sauce keeps quite well in the refrigerator, so you could actually make it several days ahead if you like.

3 large pears, cored, peeled, and cut into quarters
¾ cup port
¼ cup water
6 tablespoons honey
Grated rind of ½ large lemon
3 tablespoons fresh lemon juice

Put the pears in a small saucepan. Mix the remaining ingredients and pour over the pears. Simmer until fork-tender. Remove the pears with a slotted spoon and put in the bowl of a food processor. Reduce the liquid to a little over ½ cup. Add a tablespoon or two to the pears (reserve the rest) and purée. Refrigerate.

Serves 6

MUSTARD GREENS

In some areas it is hard to find mustard greens. But if you like them and have a little piece of sunny garden plot, they are remarkably easy to grow, being ready to harvest in as little as six weeks. I keep them going in my garden all summer. As one batch is used, I just plant another. Incidentally, greens freeze exceptionally well.

3 pounds mustard greens
2 large onions, coarsely chopped
6 ounces salt pork

After soaking the greens in a large pan of water to get rid of any sand, change the water, washing out any sand that may have settled to the bottom of the pan. Strip the leaves from the stems and discard the stems. Put the onions and salt pork in a large pot and put in the greens with just the water clinging to them. Cover and simmer for about 45 minutes. May be served with chopped green onions on top and a sprinkling of hot pepper vinegar.*

Serves 6

*To serve greens with a sprinkling of hot pepper vinegar, simply buy an inexpensive bottle of red wine vinegar, pour a little out, and stuff in whole red peppers. This must mature for about a week, but it gives all greens and dried beans extra zip.

CHEESE SPOON BREAD

There are probably as many recipes for spoon bread as there are for corn bread. Because the egg whites are beaten separately, this one is more like a soufflé than a bread. If you are concerned about getting everything finished at the same time—and then getting everyone to the table before the "soufflé" sinks—you could just serve corn bread instead. But you should have one or the other. I just can't imagine having greens without some version of baked cornmeal. Their flavors and textures are made for each other.

2 cups milk
1 scant cup cornmeal
½ teaspoon salt
2 tablespoons sugar (optional)
1 tablespoon unsalted butter
6 ounces sharp Cheddar cheese, grated
2 teaspoons baking powder
4 eggs, separated

Preheat the oven to 375 degrees.

Scald the milk in a medium saucepan. Stir the cornmeal into the milk off the heat. Over a very low flame, whisk for 2 minutes. Stir in the salt, sugar, and butter. Mix. Add the grated cheese and mix thoroughly. Let cool slightly.

Grease a 1½-quart soufflé pan. Sprinkle the baking powder over the meal mixture and incorporate it. Beat in the egg yolks. Beat the egg whites until stiff and mix in with the other ingredients, using an over-and-under motion. Pour into the soufflé pan and bake for 30 minutes, or until puffy and golden.

Serves 6

MINT JULEP ICE CREAM

I've never been too keen on bourbon in mixed drinks, but I find it especially good to cook with—which is how I came up with this ice cream.

2 cups milk
4 egg yolks
½ cup sugar
Pinch of salt
1 teaspoon finely grated vanilla bean or
2 teaspoons vanilla extract
½ cup bourbon
4 large fresh mint leaves
2 cups heavy cream

Scald the milk in a small saucepan and set aside. In a heavy-bottomed pan mix the egg yolks, sugar, and salt thoroughly. Very slowly pour in the hot milk and stir. Cook over very low heat until the mixture thickens, stirring all the while. Add the vanilla and set aside to cool. Heat the bourbon just to a simmer and drop in the mint leaves. Set aside. When egg-milk mixture is cool, strain it. Discard mint leaves and stir in the bourbon. Refrigerate.

When ready to use, add the cream and mix. Pour into an ice-cream freezer and freeze according to the manufacturer's directions.

Makes 3 pints

I think you will find the timing of this menu to be extremely flexible. The only thing that should be eaten as soon as it finishes cooking is the spoon bread. And even it will still taste good if it has to wait—it just won't look as attractive.

You may begin several days in advance if you like; in fact, the pear sauce must be made at least the day before so you will have the liquid from it to use as the base for your ham marinade. So make the sauce up to three days ahead. While you are at it, you might just as well mix the marinade and store it in the refrigerator until you need it.

The evening before the dinner, put the ham steaks in the marinade and refrigerate them, covered. They have to be turned only once—sometime the next morning. Also, remind yourself to take them out of the refrigerator several hours early so they can come to room temperature (still in the marinade). This is something you should do with all meat before you cook it. The same can be said for anything from the refrigerator that is going to be cooked in the oven.

The good news about greens is that they may be cooked several hours early and reheated. They have such a durable (I was trying not to use the word "tough") texture that they can take more reheating than more fragile vegetables.

Ice cream should also be made in the afternoon, so that it can mature in the refrigerator freezer.

So everything is done except the ham and bread, and these can bake together. Simplicity itself. Time the ham to come out about 10 minutes before the bread, to give it a few minutes to rest.

Trend Pacific wood and stainless steel flatware; Lee Bailey bar glass; Conran's dessert glass (page 7); Taitu burgundy/brown porcelain plate; Frank McIntosh gray linen napkin.

Sunny Summer Salad Lunch

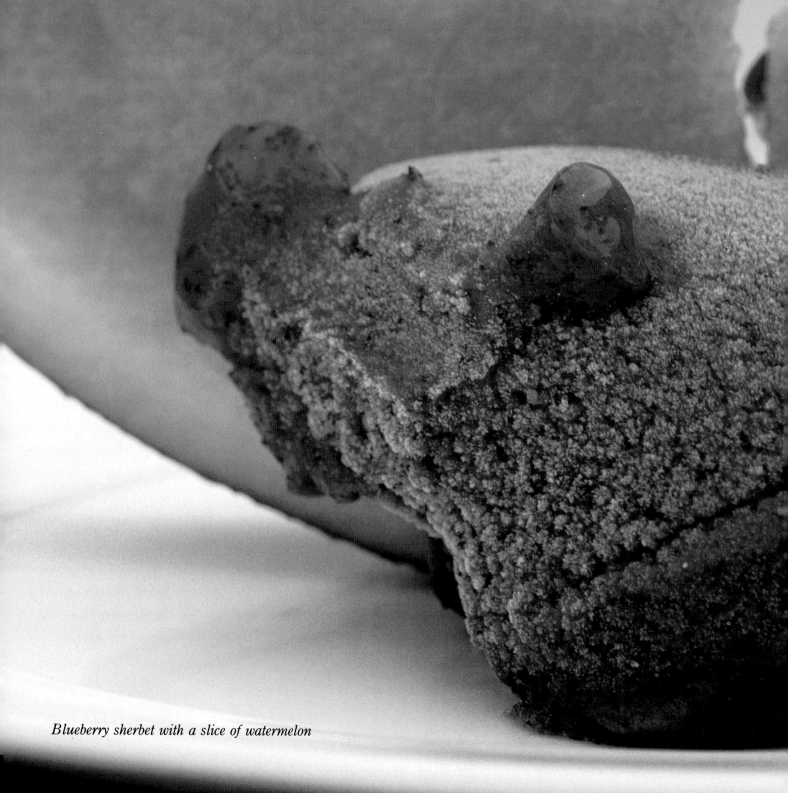

Blueberry sherbet with a slice of watermelon

Scrambled egg salad and green tomato ratatouille

Once the house (and kitchen) gets running, lunches become increasingly easy to prepare—primarily because after the first several weeks I usually have things in the refrigerator that can go into making the meal, freeing me from having to cook everything from scratch. Of course, this influences the kind of food I serve. For instance, it is probable that the green tomato ratatouille would be on hand and I would have the dough for the angel biscuits at the ready as well. As for the blueberry sherbet, I often make various ices and sherbets while berries are plentiful and at their prime.

If I'm not in the mood to make biscuits, I'll have a long loaf of French bread or toast instead. The same is true of the blueberry sherbet—if I didn't already have it, I would more than likely give everyone a slice of watermelon on a big plate and be done with it.

On the other hand, should the day be gloomy outside, I am perfectly content to spend more time in the kitchen. If you know your guests well, you might even get a couple of them in there with you to help and let it become a group effort. This can lift everyone's spirits. However, in that case we would have to call this "Gloomy Summer Salad Lunch." Doesn't sound too terrific.

MENU

Scrambled Egg Salad
Green Tomato Ratatouille
Angel Biscuits
Blueberry Sherbet with Watermelon
Wine and Iced Tea
Coffee

SCRAMBLED EGG SALAD

This salad is a good alternative to the more typical egg salad and may be served either slightly warm or slightly chilled. I'm beginning to lean more in the direction of slightly chilled. Either way, it doesn't take too much time to put together.

I have been meaning to include pine nuts in this sometime, because I like them in plain chopped egg salad. I keep forgetting to, but you might give it a try.

½ pound thick-sliced Canadian bacon
1 large sweet red pepper, roasted (see page 121), peeled, and cut into large dice
1 bunch green onions (with some top), cut into rings
1 tablespoon capers, drained and dried
½ teaspoon salt
¼ teaspoon black pepper
2 tablespoons apple cider vinegar
2 tablespoons olive oil
2 tablespoons safflower oil
4 drops Tabasco sauce
2 tablespoons mayonnaise
12 eggs, lightly beaten

Starting in a cold skillet, fry the bacon to the degree of doneness you like. Drain it on paper towels, cut into strips or dice, and put in a salad bowl. While the bacon is frying you can have the red pepper roasting. When it is roasted and diced, put it in with the bacon. Next add the onions and capers.

Make the dressing in a small bowl. Mix together the salt, pepper, and vinegar. Whisk in the oils and add the Tabasco sauce. If you are not going to serve the salad right away, stop here. If you are ready to go, add the mayonnaise and mix. Set aside while you scramble the eggs.

I use a nonstick pan coated with vegetable cooking spray to do the eggs in, and I scramble them in two batches. The trick is to have the pan fairly hot, then put in half the eggs and stir them around briefly until they set. Do the same with the other half. What you don't want to do is put them in a skillet that is not hot enough; that way they take too long to set and must be stirred too much, resulting in a mealy texture. You should have to chop the eggs after you scramble them.

So chop the eggs and add to the other ingredients in the salad bowl. Toss thoroughly but carefully. Add the dressing and toss again. Correct the seasoning if necessary.

Serves 6

GREEN TOMATO RATATOUILLE

Of all the variations on basic ratatouille, this is my favorite. I remembered someone once telling me of having had ratatouille made with green tomatoes, so when I had green tomatoes in the garden I decided to give it a try. This is what I came up with. I like it so well that the last time I made it I weighed everything so I could duplicate its flavor more accurately each time. I find that measuring by weight is much more reliable.

6 tablespoons olive oil
1 pound green tomatoes, very coarsely chopped
1 large green pepper (approximately ½ pound), coarsely chopped
3 very large garlic cloves, minced
1 pound onions, very coarsely chopped
1¾ pounds ripe tomatoes, coarsely chopped
1 pound zucchini, cut into medium-thin rounds
1 tablespoon salt
1 teaspoon black pepper
⅛ teaspoon crushed red pepper
½ teaspoon dried basil

Heat the olive oil in a large skillet and add the green tomatoes, green pepper, garlic, and onions. Sauté, stirring lightly, for 7 or 8 minutes, or until the vegetables are nicely wilted. Add the ripe tomatoes and zucchini. Cook until they are tender and have given up a lot of liquid. Add the remaining ingredients and mix carefully. Continue to simmer, at a higher heat, until most of the liquid has evaporated and what is left has thickened. Keep stirring and scraping the bottom of the pan so the vegetables don't stick or scorch.

May be served slightly warm or at room temperature. To reheat, use a double boiler.

Serves 6

ANGEL BISCUITS

These biscuits are just a variation of the old icebox rolls. The dough can be used this way or to make sweet rolls. If it tastes too sweet as it is here, you may leave out all but 1 tablespoon of sugar.

1 package dry yeast
2 tablespoons warm water
5 cups flour
4 tablespoons sugar
1 teaspoon baking powder
1 teaspoon baking soda
1½ teaspoons salt

8 tablespoons (1 stick) each unsalted
  butter and margarine
2 cups buttermilk
  Extra melted butter

Sprinkle the yeast over the warm water in a small bowl. Sift together the flour, sugar, baking powder, baking soda, and salt. In the meantime, melt the butter and margarine over a very low flame or a "flame tamer"—you do not want it to brown.

Put the sifted dry ingredients in a large bowl and add the yeast. Mix. (This will not mix very well, but that is all right.) Next add the butter-margarine and buttermilk. Mix carefully. You will wind up with a very sticky dough. Cover this with a dish towel and refrigerate until you are ready to use it.

To make the biscuits, preheat the oven to 400 degrees.

Take out a third of the dough and knead it on a floured surface for about 10 minutes. This is important, because the kneading heats up the dough and starts the yeast working.

Roll out as you would ordinary biscuits, to about ½ inch thick. Fold each one over and pinch it shut. Brush with additional melted butter and place on a generously greased cookie sheet. Bake for about 12 minutes until golden.

Makes slightly more than 3 dozen biscuits

BLUEBERRY SHERBET WITH WATERMELON

The last time I made this ice I had some coconut milk left over in the freezer, so I used that instead of water. It gave the ice a very subtle aftertaste. However, if you don't have any coconut milk handy, it is not worth the difference to justify going out to get it. Just use water.

¾ cup coconut milk
½ cup sugar
1 teaspoon lemon juice
1 pint fresh blueberries, puréed
6 small watermelon slices

Combine the coconut milk, sugar, and lemon juice in a saucepan and bring to a boil. Turn off the heat. When cool, add to the puréed blueberries. Mix well and freeze in an automatic ice-cream maker according to the manufacturer's directions or in the freezer compartment of your refrigerator (see page 21).

Serve with a small slice of cold watermelon.

Serves 6

The biscuits could be made days in advance, as the dough will keep for up to a week in the refrigerator. I am also assuming that blueberry sherbet is something you already have in your freezer.

The ratatouille could be made anytime in the morning and left out, lightly covered with a dish towel, until you want it.

Make the scrambled egg salad about 20 minutes before you plan to serve it, so it can chill just slightly. The biscuits can be kneaded and baked while the salad is chilling. Otherwise, there isn't too much to do here.

Incidentally, for those who don't want to eat too many eggs, you may cheat a little by leaving out a couple of the eggs and discarding a couple of the yolks of the ones you do use. Stretch the salad a bit by adding tomatoes. This would be slightly redundant with the green tomato ratatouille, but the tomatoes in that dish have a completely different flavor from the raw ones.

Yamazaki stainless steel flatware; Williams-Sonoma tall glass tumbler; Taitu for Tiffany white plate with thin royal blue band; D. F. Sanders blue/gray linen napkin.

Oven-fried fish with fennel and corn

Oven Fish Fry

Raspberry-apple pudding topped with cream

One of my favorite ways to prepare fish is to fry it. This can be a bit messy, however, especially the spattering and coping with the leftover oil. So here is a method whereby you can have your fish fry almost without the mess. It requires comparatively little time, and is typically served with tartar sauce (or homemade catsup).

Accompanying the fish are old-fashioned skillet corn and fennel Niçoise, which has an interesting flavor. An English-style summer pudding rounds it all off.

OVEN-FRIED FISH

You may use almost any kind of firm whitefish for this, from fluke to bass. I think the breading of the fillets is best done just before you cook them—although some people say that the fish may be breaded in advance and refrigerated.

    Flour for dredging
1 egg, lightly beaten with 3 tablespoons milk
    Fresh bread crumbs
6 whitefish fillets (totaling just under 2 pounds), all the same size if possible
    Salt to taste
    Black pepper to taste
½ cup (1 stick) unsalted butter, melted

Garnish
    Capers
    Lemon slices

Preheat the oven to 500 degrees.

Lay out a piece of waxed paper and put the flour for dredging on it. Next to it put a shallow plate for the egg-milk mixture. Last, lay out another sheet of waxed paper for the bread crumbs. Dredge the fillets in the flour, shaking off any excess. Dip them in the egg mixture and let the excess drain off. Finally, coat with bread crumbs, pressing gently to make them adhere. Salt and pepper the top of the fish generously.

Line with foil a pan that is large enough to hold all the fillets in one layer. Put half of the butter in it and place in the oven. Let it heat for 4 or 5 minutes. Do not let it burn. Remove the pan from the oven and immediately place the fillets in it, seasoned side down. Pour the remaining butter over all. Salt and pepper the top. Bake for about 10 minutes, or until the fish flakes easily and is lightly browned. If you like it browner, run it under the broiler for just a couple of minutes—watching it all the while so it does not burn.

Garnish with a sprinkling of capers and the lemon slices.

Serves 6

TARTAR SAUCE

There are lots of ingredients that can go into tartar sauce: chives, red onion, celery salt, chopped olives, pimiento, and horseradish to name a few. My feeling about this is that there is a point of diminishing returns, where one flavor begins to cancel out another. I like a lot of onion and dill and less capers and pickle. The best bet is to choose a combination and proportions that you like, but limit the ingredients to four or five.

8 tablespoons mayonnaise (preferably homemade)
4 tablespoons plain yogurt
2 teaspoons fresh lemon juice
4 drops Tabasco sauce
¼ teaspoon black pepper
    Salt to taste
    Chopped green onion, sweet pickle, dill, and/or small capers

Mix the mayonnaise and yogurt together thoroughly and add the lemon juice, Tabasco sauce, pepper, and salt. Stir in the remaining ingredients.

Makes approximately 1 cup

FENNEL NIÇOISE

Fennel is a vegetable that I don't cook very often, mostly using it raw in salad, but this recipe is awfully good. It can be prepared earlier in the day and reheated. It doesn't have to be very hot—I like it best just warm.

8 fennel bulbs
2 tablespoons unsalted butter
4 tablespoons olive oil
2 medium onions, thinly sliced
2 large garlic cloves, thoroughly crushed
2 pounds tomatoes, skinned, seeded, and cut into chunks
2 tablespoons fresh lemon juice
2 tablespoons wine vinegar
1 heaping tablespoon tomato paste
¼ teaspoon dried thyme or 1 sprig fresh thyme
¼ teaspoon salt
¼ teaspoon black pepper
2 green onions (with some top), chopped
1 tablespoon very finely chopped fresh parsley
1 cup small Niçoise olives

Trim the fennel, removing any tough outer layers as well as the piece of root at the end. Cut into ½-inch slices. Melt the butter in a large skillet and sauté the fennel, covered, for 15 minutes or less, just until tender. Remove from the pan and set aside.

Add the olive oil to the pan, and when it is hot add the onions and garlic. Sauté, uncovered, until they have wilted. Add the tomatoes and simmer until most of their liquid has evaporated. Mix in the lemon juice, vinegar, tomato paste, thyme, salt, pepper, green onions, and parsley. Cover and simmer until the liquid is reduced. Add the fennel and cook for a few more minutes before adding the olives. Correct the seasoning if necessary.

Serves 6

SKILLET CORN

The taste of corn prepared this way sends me right back to my childhood. It's important to cook the corn long enough for it to start turning slightly golden and develop a nutty flavor. If I remember correctly, sometimes it was combined with chopped sweet red pepper, but I like it better plain.

2 tablespoons safflower oil
1 tablespoon unsalted butter
1 tablespoon bacon fat
  Corn kernels cut from 10 ears of corn
  (scrape the cob for juice)
  Salt to taste (optional)

Heat the oil, butter, and fat in a large skillet until very hot. Add the corn quickly, stirring to coat all the kernels. Continue to stir as it cooks, later scraping up any that sticks to the bottom. Sample it after a few minutes to test for doneness; cooking time will depend on the age and kind of corn. Add salt if desired.

Serves 6

RASPBERRY-APPLE SUMMER PUDDING

I have a real weakness for fruit desserts. This one is a favorite that I started serving several years ago. The technique is really quite simple, but if you have never prepared one before it may take a second try to get it to come out properly. But the pudding tastes good even if it's a little too dry or too soupy.

1 pound raspberries
1 large Granny Smith apple, cored, peeled, and sliced
  Grated rind of 1 lemon
6 tablespoons sugar
  Approximately 5 slices cinnamon raisin bread
  Heavy cream flavored with vanilla extract

Put the raspberries, apple, lemon rind, and sugar in a saucepan. Cover and simmer for 10 minutes. Keep an eye on this, as it can overflow when it boils up.

Trim the crusts from the bread and cut the slices to line the bottom and sides of a 4-cup soufflé dish. Strain the fruit pulp, reserving the juice. Pour several tablespoons of juice over the bottom slices of bread and let set for a few minutes, until it is absorbed. Fill the dish almost to the top with fruit pulp and add just a little more juice. Cover the top completely with the remaining bread slices. Put a small plate on top that just fits inside the dish and wrap with plastic film. Set on a plate in the refrigerator and weight the top. (A large can may be used as a weight.) Leave for 24 hours.

Run a knife around the edges and invert the dish onto a serving platter, being careful not to spill the accumulated juice. If the juice has not stained all the bread through, you may do so with the reserved juice. Serve with cream (whipped or not) and extra juice.

Serves 6

GAME PLAN

You will have to start the pudding the day before to give it time to set in the refrigerator overnight. The good thing about this is that it will be done and out of the way. You will only have to add a bit of vanilla to the heavy cream and you will be done.

On the day of the meal, you might make the fennel Niçoise toward the end of the afternoon and set it aside. You don't have to refrigerate it unless you must make it very early in the day. As reheating a dish often overcooks it, you might just serve it warm, which is easily accomplished by letting it sit on the back of the stove, covered with a dish towel, while you work.

Corn may be cut off the cob a few hours in advance and finished while the fish is baking. This way, they will probably come out at the same time. If your timing doesn't quite jibe, the corn can wait for a bit without being any the worse for it.

So the fish is prepared last. Unlike the other dishes, it really should be served hot.

Tartar sauce could be made whenever you can find a spare moment, then refrigerated. If you can remember to do so, you might take it out of the refrigerator an hour before you want to use it, so it won't be so cold.

Christofle silverplate flatware; Simon Pearce hand-blown Irish glass; Limoges porcelain plate; Frank McIntosh grape linen napkin.

Special Summer Lunch

Above: *Pasta sausage garnished with lemon rind and served with green sauce*
Below: *The sausage, wrapped for cooking (left) and ready to serve (right)*

Most of the time in the country, lunches are put together in the least complicated way—from whatever is in the refrigerator. I am partial to cheeses and bread with olives, tomatoes, and good tuna in olive oil, so this makes noontime easy. And in a pinch I am perfectly happy with a plain tomato sandwich, provided that the tomatoes are vine-ripened and the mayonnaise is homemade.

However, there are occasions when you have special guests, or are just in the mood to cook something different. This is a menu for such times.

The pasta sausage is delicious with its fresh-tasting sauce, and makes a very appetizing presentation. It is accompanied simply by buttered steamed asparagus, hard-boiled eggs, olives and tomatoes, and whatever other things you might have on hand—such as roasted peppers in oil, wilted onions, and the like.

MENU

Pasta Sausage
Uncooked Green Sauce
Steamed Asparagus
Tomatoes, Olives, Eggs
Cantaloupe Ice with Blueberries
Wine and Iced Tea
Coffee

Cantaloupe ice on a bed of blueberries

PASTA SAUSAGE

One of the best things about this dish, aside from the way it tastes and looks on the plate, is that it does not have to be served piping hot—so long as it is not refrigerator-cold, it is fine.

Incidentally, this recipe looks complicated, but in fact it is quite the opposite. Read it over once and visualize what it is you are doing and all will be fine.

One 12 × 15-inch sheet of fresh pasta*
2 tablespoons (¼ stick) unsalted butter
½ cup diced boiled ham
4 large green onions, finely chopped
1 ounce dried mushrooms, soaked, patted dry, and coarsely chopped
5 ounces stemmed fresh or frozen spinach, steamed and squeezed dry
8 ounces cream cheese, at room temperature
¼ cup Parmesan cheese
Generous ½ cup ricotta cheese
1 egg
⅛ teaspoon white pepper
3 tablespoons finely chopped parsley
3 ounces prosciutto, sliced
Melted butter for sealing edges
Chicken stock

Garnish
Thin strips from rind of 1 lemon

Lay out the pasta on a sheet of waxed paper. Cover with another sheet of waxed paper and set aside.

Melt the butter and add the ham, green onions, and mushrooms. Sauté for 3 minutes. Mix in the spinach. Set aside. In another bowl, beat together the cream cheese, Parmesan, and ricotta. Add the egg, pepper, parsley, and ham mixture. Mix well.

Spread the mixture on the pasta sheet, leaving a 2-inch border at one of the short ends. Arrange the prosciutto on top of that. Brush the edge with melted butter. Roll up the pasta like a jelly roll. Wrap it in a doubled piece of cheesecloth. Tie the ends very securely.

Fill a large kettle (or a fish poacher) with chicken stock and bring to a boil. Place the pasta roll in the stock and simmer gently for 25 minutes. Remove and drain. Let it rest for a few minutes before carefully removing the cheesecloth. Garnish with strips of lemon rind. Slice into ½-inch pieces after the roll has cooled slightly, making sure each portion has a few lemon strips on top. The taste of lemon rind is a very pleasant addition of flavor. So far as I am concerned, edible

garnishes that enhance the taste of the dish are a must whenever possible. Serve with Uncooked Green Sauce (recipe follows).

Serves 8

*You can buy sheets of pasta fresh at some Italian markets and specialty shops. They are also available frozen, in which case let them thaw out before using them. If you cannot find a 12 × 15-inch sheet, join two sheets by overlapping them slightly, dampening the seam where they join, and then pressing them together.

UNCOOKED GREEN SAUCE

You must correct the flavor of this sauce to your own taste after you have finished puréeing all the ingredients together. Often it will need a bit more salt and pepper or oil and vinegar. Let your taste buds be your guide.

It should always be served at room temperature, but refrigerate any that is left over. Let it come back to room temperature before using it again.

This is also useful as a sauce for poached fish, as well as hot pasta. Toss the pasta with a bit of butter first, then sauce, then grated Parmesan cheese and peeled, seeded, and diced tomatoes. The tomatoes will need a bit more salt.

1 slice dense white bread (such as Tuscan bread)
3 tablespoons wine vinegar
1 large shallot, peeled
4 large green onions (with some top)
1 small garlic clove, peeled
1 medium tomato, peeled and seeded
1 small cucumber, peeled and seeded
3 tablespoons chopped fresh parsley (without stems)
4 flat anchovy fillets
2 tablespoons capers, drained, rinsed, and dried
2 tablespoons olive oil
2 tablespoons safflower oil
1 tablespoon green peppercorn mustard
Tabasco sauce to taste
¾ teaspoon salt
½ teaspoon black pepper

Put the bread in a deep saucer and pour the vinegar over it. Coarsely chop all the vegetables and put them in a food processor, along with the remaining ingredients. Add the soaked bread and any vinegar that was not absorbed. Process to a fine purée, stopping to scrape down the sides several times.

Makes approximately 2 cups

STEAMED ASPARAGUS

Gauge the number of asparagus stalks you will need by their size. The ones pictured were very large, so I needed only three per serving. After washing the asparagus thoroughly, peel the skin off the lower, tender end of the stem (cut off the tough white portion of the stem, if there is any). Steam them to the degree of doneness you like. I prefer mine just fork-tender, not undercooked.

TOMATOES, OLIVES, EGGS

The tomatoes should be peeled but not seeded. I dip them in boiling water for about 30 seconds—even briefer if the tomatoes are really ripe—then refrigerate them, unpeeled, to wait until I am ready to serve them. An assortment of green and black olives (in oil) should be at room temperature.

A word here about hard-boiled eggs (allow 1 per guest). Peeling them after they have been boiled is easier if the eggs were punctured at one end before cooking, either with a pin or with an ingenious and inexpensive little device sold just for this purpose (see "Gadgets," page 140). When they are done, immediately plunge them into cold water. This makes the cooked egg contract, so that it does not adhere to the inside of the shell—which can make peeling them so tedious a task.

CANTALOUPE ICE WITH BLUEBERRIES

It is very easy to make this if you have an ice-cream freezer. Even if you don't, it can be done in the refrigerator freezer—if you can find the room. Otherwise, give up and buy the ice ready-made. That is certainly what I would do in the city in any case.

> 1¼ cups Simple Syrup (see page 97)
> 3½ cups cantaloupe purée (approximately 1 large cantaloupe)
> 1 tablespoon fresh lemon juice
> Grated rind of ½ lemon
> 1 pint blueberries

Chill all the ingredients, then combine syrup, purée, and lemon juice and rind. Pour into a metal pan. Place in the freezer, covered. When it is almost frozen, put it in a food processor and give it a few quick whirls. Put it back in the pan, cover, and repeat the process once more after it is almost frozen again. Let it rest

for about an hour before serving. If you have neither an ice-cream freezer nor a food processor, you can do the aerating in a blender.

Serve the ice on a bed of blueberries.

About 3 cups

GAME PLAN

To prepare this lunch, I would make the sauce first; it can stand out at room temperature for several hours. Then I would tackle the pasta sausage. You should time yourself so that the sausage comes out of its cooking liquid about when your guests are to arrive.

While this is simmering, you might dip the tomatoes and put them in the refrigerator. Also get the asparagus ready, so that you will only have to turn on the heat under them just before serving. Boil the eggs anytime.

The ice should go into the freezer enough ahead of time so it can be waiting before the guests are ready for their dessert. Of course, the blueberries would have been washed and refrigerated before as well.

Don't forget to have the olives at room temperature, too, if they were in the refrigerator.

Should the green sauce not appeal to you, serve the pasta slices with your own favorite light tomato sauce. If you decide to do this, eliminate the fresh tomato as garnish. And if the ice seems like too much trouble to prepare and a good commercial one is not to be found, have blueberries with cream, sprinkled with brown sugar.

Georg Jensen for Royal Copenhagen sterling silver flatware; Sven Jensen wineglass; Pottery Barn matte stone bisque plate; Bailey-Bannett Inc. glass dessert bowl (page 19); D. F. Sanders linen napkin.

Lamb steak with chutney, rice,
and vegetable purée

Strawberry cake topped with strawberry preserves

Grilled Outdoor Supper

Baked Italian rice

For many people summer entertaining is synonymous with cooking outdoors on the grill. Admittedly, this is a very convivial way of doing things; it seems to invite people to stand around and talk good-naturedly while they watch the host being enveloped in smoke. But if he doesn't mind, why should we? Still others never grill anything more than an occasional hot dog for the kids. I suppose I fall someplace in the middle. When I cook outside, it is seldom anything other than meat grilled over charcoal or mesquite (or whatever chic smoke is in vogue at the time).

I have a real weakness for charcoaled lamb, so this meal is centered around that favorite of mine. Instead of having the leg butterflied, I have it cut into steaks. They are accompanied by baked Italian rice and a vegetable purée. For dessert, there is a cake made with strawberries. This rounds out what seems to me an appealing down-home meal. I always serve it with corn bread, but do as you like.

Charcoaled Bourbon-Marinated
Lamb Steaks
Baked Italian Rice
Carrots and Baked Onions Purée
(page 121)
Strawberry Cake with Refrigerator
Strawberry Preserves
Wine or Beer
Coffee

CHARCOALED BOURBON-MARINATED LAMB STEAKS

I order a medium-size leg of lamb for this and have the butcher cut ½-inch steaks from it (across the bone). The number you get depends on the size of the leg, but it is always enough to serve eight, and sometimes a little more. But cook them all, because they are good cold, sliced thin. There should be enough marinade to cover all the meat. If there isn't, slightly increase the amount called for.

  1 medium leg of lamb, approximately 8 pounds,
    cut into ½-inch steaks
1½ cups bourbon
  ¾ cup soy sauce
  ¾ cup olive oil
  3 large garlic cloves, chopped
  3 large onions, thinly sliced

Garnish
    Chutney
    Mustard
    Slivered green onions

Put the lamb steaks in a glass or plastic container large enough to hold them comfortably. Combine the remaining ingredients and pour over the lamb. Cover and refrigerate for 24 hours, or a little longer. Now and then give the steaks a turn.

About an hour before you want to start cooking, take the steaks out of the refrigerator and let them come to room temperature.

Arrange the charcoal in the grill so that you have a large even bed. After it is lighted, give it 30 to 40 minutes, so that all the coals are covered with a good gray ash. Put the meat on and set your timer for 7 minutes. Turn the steaks and give them another 7 minutes. They will be slightly pink inside, but not bloody. If anyone wants his very pink, give that steak 5 minutes per side.

Serve with chutney and mustard, and I like mine with a good bite of green onion.

Serves 8

BAKED ITALIAN RICE

This is really a very simple dish, but it requires that you make a portion of risotto first, and in order to do that properly you should use only Arborio rice. This is a type of rice used in Italy, different from our American kind. It is available in many Italian markets and specialty stores. Incidentally, any variation of basic risotto may be substituted.

  6 cups rich chicken stock
  4 tablespoons (½ stick) unsalted butter
  1 medium onion, finely chopped
  2 cups Arborio rice
  ½ cup dry white wine
    Salt to taste
  3 eggs, lightly beaten
  6 ounces Gruyère cheese, coarsely grated

Preheat the oven to 400 degrees and put the stock in a pot on the stove to warm slowly.

Heat half the butter in a heavy saucepan and sauté the onion until it is translucent. Add the rice and coat well with butter. Stir for a few seconds, then add the wine. When it evaporates, start adding stock to the rice, ½ cup at a time. Stir it well after each addition of stock and once or twice as it is being absorbed. You want this to be just barely simmering, not boiling. Repeat until all the stock has been absorbed and the mixture is al dente and creamy. Add the rest of the butter and let the rice rest while you lightly grease a 1½-quart casserole or flat pan. Add the eggs to the rice and mix well, leaving no lumps. Add salt to taste. Pour half of it into the casserole and cover it with the grated cheese. Top with the remaining rice. Smooth this over and bake for 40 minutes, or until the top begins to turn golden.

If you would like to serve this unmolded instead of spooned out, let it cool for about 5 minutes and then run a knife around the edges and invert onto a serving plate.

Serves 8

STRAWBERRY CAKE

This is a marvelous mess of a cake, in the same juicy way an English trifle is a mess. It is very moist, and the preserves it is topped with have a different flavor from the berries cooked in the cake. This recipe presupposes that you have the refrigerator strawberry preserves on hand. Regular preserves can be used, but they are sweeter and have to be melted with a small amount of water to make their consistency a little runny.

      3 cups hulled and halved strawberries
    1½ cups sugar
      1 tablespoon unsalted butter, melted
      4 eggs, separated
          Pinch of salt
      1 teaspoon cream of tartar
      1 teaspoon vanilla extract
      1 cup sifted flour
          Refrigerator Strawberry Preserves (recipe follows)

Garnish
          Whole hulled strawberries
          Whipped cream or ice cream

Preheat the oven to 325 degrees.

Very generously butter an 8- or 9-inch springform pan. Put the berries in the pan, sprinkle with ½ cup sugar, and set aside. Beat the melted (but not hot) butter into the egg yolks and set aside. Beat the egg whites with the pinch of salt, and when they are foamy add the cream of tartar. Continue beating until stiff. Fold in the remaining sugar, a little at a time, with an over-and-under motion. Mix the vanilla with the egg yolks and fold them into the egg whites. Last, fold in the flour, ¼ cup at a time. Pour over the berries in the pan and bake for 1 hour and 10 minutes, or until a cake tester comes out clean. This cake can fool you by looking quite done while it is undercooked inside.

Let cool for a few minutes, then place on a serving platter and remove the outer ring. It will give up a good bit of juice. Spoon some of it on top. Then put the preserves on top of this and let it dribble down the sides. Garnish the top with the whole berries. Serve the cake without trying to remove it from the bottom of the springform pan, as this could break the cake.

Top each portion with whipped cream or ice cream.

Serves 8 to 12

REFRIGERATOR STRAWBERRY PRESERVES

      1 pint strawberries, hulled and quartered
    ½ cup sugar
    ½ teaspoon fresh lemon juice

Alternate layers of berries and sugar in a small enameled pot and bring to a boil. Lower heat and stir from time to time. Cook for about 10 minutes and add the lemon juice. With a slotted spoon, remove the berries to a jar. Simmer the juice until reduced by half. Let cook and pour over the berries. Cover and keep refrigerated.

Makes 1 scant pint

GAME PLAN

Once the coals are right, the lamb steaks can be finished in exactly 14 minutes, and don't even have to be carved to be served. The rice can be timed to come out about when the lamb will be done, and the vegetable purée can be made and kept warm while all this is going on. Make the cake earlier in the day. Simplicity itself.

Wolfman-Gold flatware; Veralux French jelly glass; Lee Bailey white porcelain buffet plate; Frank McIntosh napkin.

Oyster Fry

Fried oysters with tartar sauce,
blackberry catsup, and tomatoes

MENU

Cornmeal Fried Oysters
Blackberry Catsup
Tartar Sauce (page 16)
Avocado Coleslaw
Pecan Sugar Cookies
Mixed Fruit
Beer or Iced Tea
Coffee

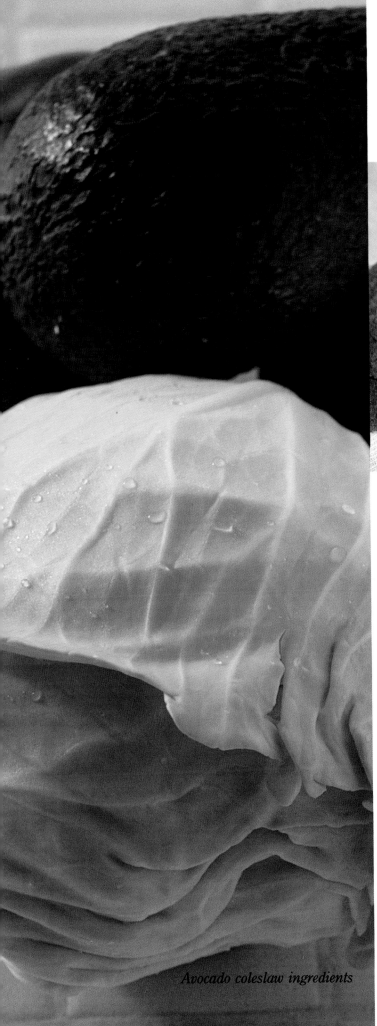

Avocado coleslaw ingredients

Fried oysters are one of my all-time favorite foods. When I was a child my family scrupulously stuck to the old belief that they should not be eaten in months that don't have an "r" in them. I realize now that this probably had more to do with oysters not being as fat in the summer and therefore not as tasty. Anyway, "r" or not, I eat fried oysters only when I can cook them in the country—my kitchen in the city is simply not well ventilated enough to fry them in, and the used oil can be a pain to get rid of.

Some years ago I bought a large pot with a fitted basket (see "Pots, Pans, and Appliances," page 136) in which I can fry several dozen oysters at a time. And although I use the pot only a few times a year, it makes the task so much easier that the investment was worth it.

You don't need too much else to make this meal if you really like oysters. Here they are accompanied by tartar sauce, blackberry catsup—a favorite of mine, and easy to make—avocado coleslaw, and sliced tomatoes. The dessert is mixed fruit with a marvelous pecan sugar cookie.

I am also including a recipe for corn and tomatoes, which would make a delicious accompaniment to the oysters too. I had planned to include this recipe in the last two cookbooks, and each time something happened to bump it out. So I figure it is now or never.

CORNMEAL FRIED OYSTERS

There are a number of ingredients such as flour, cracker crumbs, and meal, used separately or in combination, to coat oysters for frying. I have tried most of them, but for my money, you just can't beat plain cornmeal. It creates the perfect thin, crunchy casing for these delicious little morsels.

     Safflower or corn oil for frying
     Approximately 3 cups yellow cornmeal
1 tablespoon black pepper
1 teaspoon salt
6 dozen medium oysters (more if very small), shucked and drained

Put the oil in a deep fryer with a wire basket and heat to very hot. If you have a frying thermometer, the temperature should be 375 degrees.

While the oil is heating, mix the cornmeal, pepper, and salt on a long sheet of waxed paper, placed next to the stove, if possible. Drain the oysters and roll in the mixture, coating well. Put the coated oysters in a single layer in the wire basket and lower it into the hot oil. Fry a batch at a time this way for about 2 minutes, until golden. Continue until all are fried. Keep the oysters warm on paper towels in the oven (in one layer) until you finish them all. Serve immediately on a warm platter. Let the oil reheat for a few seconds between batches.

Serves 6

BLACKBERRY CATSUP

This is extremely easy to make and is so much better than commercial tomato catsup that once you try it you will be hooked. I must admit that I don't bottle it the proper way. I just sterilize the container and keep it in the refrigerator. It may stay like that for a few months. To keep it longer, you should do a correct bottling job.

2 cups blackberries
½ cup cider vinegar
½ cup water
¾ cup firmly packed dark brown sugar
½ teaspoon ground cloves
½ teaspoon ground ginger
1 teaspoon ground cinnamon
¼ teaspoon cayenne pepper
½ teaspoon salt
2 tablespoons (¼ stick) unsalted butter

Mix the berries with the vinegar and water in a saucepan. Bring to a boil, lower the heat to a simmer, cook for 5 minutes, and then sieve out the seeds. Return to the saucepan and add the remaining ingredients. Simmer for about 10 minutes, until thickened. Let cool and pour into a sterilized bottle with a tight cap.

Makes approximately 2 cups

AVOCADO COLESLAW

Here is a good variation on an old favorite. If you don't like avocados, you won't like this. In that case, try the Maque Choux recipe, below. Since there are green onions in the tartar sauce, you might want to leave them out of this recipe. I like them so well that it doesn't bother me to have them in both dishes.

2 medium avocados, peeled, pitted, and mashed
2 tablespoons plus 1 teaspoon fresh lemon juice
4 cups coarsely chopped cabbage
⅔ cup coarsely chopped green onions (with some top)
1 large sweet red pepper, roasted (see page 121), seeded, peeled, and diced
6 tablespoons mayonnaise
1 teaspoon sugar
1 tablespoon balsamic vinegar
¾ teaspoon salt
¼ teaspoon Tabasco sauce
1 teaspoon Worcestershire sauce

Mix the avocado and lemon juice thoroughly. Add the cabbage and green onions and mix. Then combine with the red pepper.

Make a dressing by whisking together all the remaining ingredients. Stir into the cabbage mixture. Cover and refrigerate.

Toss before serving.

Serves 6 to 8

CORN AND TOMATOES (MAQUE CHOUX)*

This is a very popular way of serving corn in my native Louisiana—and, because it was a favorite of my father's, a dish I have had many times. Try it when tomatoes and corn are at their best.

1 tablespoon bacon drippings
3 tablespoons unsalted butter
1 medium onion, finely chopped

4 cups fresh corn kernels, cut from the cob
2 medium tomatoes, peeled, seeded, and diced
Salt and pepper to taste

Put the bacon drippings and butter in a large skillet and sauté the onion until wilted, about 5 minutes. Do not let it brown. Add the corn and tomatoes. Simmer for about 10 minutes and season with salt and pepper. If it begins to dry out, add a few tablespoons of milk or chicken stock. Serve warm.

Serves 6 to 8

*Alternate recipe to Avocado Coleslaw

PECAN SUGAR COOKIES

These are very delicious and very thin, and should be kept in an airtight tin so the humidity won't get to them.

8 tablespoons (1 stick) margarine, softened
8 tablespoons (1 stick) unsalted butter, softened
¾ cup tightly packed brown sugar
1 egg yolk
1 tablespoon vanilla extract
1 cup finely ground pecans
¾ cup flour
¼ teaspoon salt

Preheat the oven to 350 degrees.
Cream the margarine and butter with the sugar. Add the egg yolk and vanilla and stir. Mix together the pecans, flour, and salt. Combine thoroughly with the sugar mixture. Using two teaspoons, push off a teaspoonful at a time onto an ungreased cookie sheet. Leave several inches between each dab of dough, as they spread out quite a lot, becoming paper-thin.
Bake for 9 to 11 minutes, until golden brown. Letting them get too dark will ruin their taste. The varying cooking time has to do with the accuracy of your oven and the amount of dough dropped from the teaspoon. Test just two or three cookies on a small sheet to get your timing right.
Let the cookies cool for about 3 or 4 minutes before removing them with a spatula, the end of which should be wiped off with a paper towel after you have removed several cookies. If you try to lift the cookies up too soon you will destroy their shape. If left waiting too long, they will break up when you try to remove them. All this sounds more complicated than it really is. Just do your test batch and you will get the hang of it right away.

Makes 3 dozen cookies

MIXED FRUIT

You could use any combination of fruit that you like together—or whatever is available. This is one I particularly like.

6 small peaches, peeled, pitted, and cut into big slices
1 small honeydew melon, peeled, seeded, and cut into cubes
1 large bunch champagne grapes
Fresh lemon juice, to taste

Garnish
Lime slices

Mix together the peaches, melon, and grapes and squeeze lemon juice over them. Refrigerate until ready to use. Serve with a slice of lime.

Serves 6

GAME PLAN

To prepare this meal, make the coleslaw late in the afternoon, along with the mixed fruit and tartar sauce. The cookies may be made the day before, and I am assuming you will have made the blackberry catsup at some earlier time. Plan to slice the tomatoes just before you start frying the oysters.
When you are ready to start, tell everyone that they have about 15 minutes before dinner—then get frying. The oysters should be eaten hot.

Taitu black wood with stainless steel flatware; Williams-Sonoma stemmed beer glass; Dean & Deluca earthenware mustard plate with black rim; antique jade salt and pepper serving dish (page 26); Bailey-Bannett Inc. stainless steel dessert bowl and saucer (page 27); D. F. Sanders ribbed natural linen napkin.

Fall Sunday Lunch

Sausage pasta cake

W hen the weather begins to get a bit nippy I have a favorite dish I like to make. It is a sausage-filled pasta "cake," which forms the centerpiece of a hearty menu I serve to guests on Sunday before they leave to go back to the city. This would be a little too heavy for the usual midday meal, but on Sundays I sometimes like to give friends a little more substantial repast, this often being the main meal of the day. It is accompanied by a delicious salad of green peppers and cucumbers dressed with yogurt—very low in calories—and the last of the corn. For dessert, I splurge on a few strawberries to top melon dressed with wine gelatin.

Above: *A slice of pasta sausage cake with tomato red pepper sauce*
Below: *Green pepper and cucumber salad garnished with red onions (left) Corn off the cob (right)*

Melon with wine gelatin and strawberries
garnished with mint

MENU

Sausage Pasta Cake
Tomato and Sweet Red Pepper Sauce
Green Pepper and Cucumber Salad
Corn Off the Cob
Melon with Red Wine Gelatin
and Strawberries
Wine
Coffee

SAUSAGE PASTA CAKE

This may be served right out of the oven (after it rests for about 5 minutes) or it can wait for an hour. It is quite good just warm. Any leftovers should be rewarmed slightly (covered).

Pasta
- ¾ pound spaghettini
- 3 tablespoons unsalted butter
- 1 small onion, finely chopped
- 3 tablespoons flour
- 1½ cups hot chicken stock
- ¼ teaspoon white pepper
- 1 teaspoon fresh lemon juice
- 6 tablespoons Parmesan cheese, freshly grated
- 1 cup grated mild Cheddar cheese
- 3 large eggs
- ½ teaspoon salt

Filling
- ¾ pound sausage meat
- 1 tablespoon unsalted butter
- 1 tablespoon safflower oil
- ¾ cup coarsely chopped green peppers
- 1¾ cups coarsely chopped onions
- ⅓ cup grated mild Cheddar cheese
- 3 tablespoons chopped fresh parsley
- ½ teaspoon black pepper

Preheat the oven to 375 degrees. Generously butter a springform pan (such as a cheesecake pan) and sprinkle with bread crumbs. Set aside.

Put the pasta in a large pot of boiling salted water. Cook at a rolling boil for 7 minutes. Drain and run cold water over it. Set aside.

Put the sausage meat in a cold skillet and brown it slowly, separating it into a crumbly mixture.

While that is going on, make a white sauce for the pasta by melting the butter in a skillet and browning the chopped onion. Then add the flour and mix well. Slowly pour in the heated stock, and continue to simmer for a few minutes until the mixture thickens. Add the white pepper and lemon juice.

In a large bowl combine the pasta, sauce, Parmesan cheese, Cheddar cheese, eggs, and salt. Mix well. Set aside for a few minutes.

Remove the browned sausage meat from the skillet and pour out any fat. Wipe out the skillet and add the butter and safflower oil. Sauté the green peppers and onions until they are limp and add this to the meat, along with the Cheddar cheese, parsley, and black pepper. Mix well.

To assemble the dish, put half the pasta mixture in the pan. Make a deep depression in the middle, leaving a ½ inch space around the edges. Heap the meat mixture into the depression, mounding it in the middle. Pat it down solidly. Place the rest of the pasta on top and smooth it over. Top with any leftover bread crumbs and dot with butter.

Bake for 35 or 40 minutes, until the top is brown. Let stand for a few minutes before removing the outside ring of the pan. Do not bother to remove the bottom. Serve with Tomato and Sweet Red Pepper Sauce (recipe follows).

Serves 8 generously

TOMATO AND SWEET RED PEPPER SAUCE

This has a marvelous flavor and can be used anytime you need a rich tomato sauce.

- 3½ pounds ripe tomatoes
- 3 medium garlic cloves
- 2 tablespoons unsalted butter
- 2 tablespoons safflower oil
- 3 large onions, coarsely chopped
- 16 fresh tarragon leaves
- 15 parsley sprigs (without stems), finely chopped
- 1 very large red pepper, roasted (see page 121), peeled, and seeded
- 1 teaspoon salt
- ¼ teaspoon black pepper
- 2 tablespoons tomato paste

Dip the tomatoes in hot water for 40 seconds. Skin and seed them. Set aside. Peel the garlic and cut each clove in half. Heat the oil and butter in a large skillet and add the garlic. Mashing down on the pieces, sauté it until it starts to brown, then remove and discard it. Sauté the onions until they are translucent and then add the tomato pulp and tarragon leaves. Simmer for 30 minutes. Add the parsley and simmer for another 10 minutes. Purée in a food processor (this may be either smooth or coarse) and return it to the pan. Purée the red pepper, add it and the salt, black pepper, and tomato paste to the sauce, and simmer for 5 minutes.

Makes approximately 4 cups

GREEN PEPPER AND CUCUMBER SALAD

This salad is quite easy to prepare. Just be sure to give the cucumbers enough time to give up their water, or the whole thing can get too liquid.

2 very large green peppers, roasted (see page 121), peeled, and seeded
2 large cucumbers, peeled, seeded, and cut into thick slices
1 teaspoon salt
6 tablespoons plain yogurt
3 tablespoons wine vinegar
¼ teaspoon black pepper
½ teaspoon sugar
1 medium garlic clove, cut in half
½ small red onion, sliced into thin rinds

Cut the roasted peppers into strips and then into large dice. Set aside.

Put the cucumber slices in a bowl and salt them generously. Refrigerate for at least an hour. When you are ready to use them, drain them and squeeze between paper towels to dry.

Make a dressing by combining the remaining ingredients except the onion rings. Mix the cucumbers and pepper and pour the dressing over all. Just before serving, remove the garlic and stir. Top with thin rings of red onion.

Serves 6.

CORN OFF THE COB

While fresh corn on the cob quickly steamed or boiled and slathered with butter certainly must be one of our national favorites, I must confess I prefer it cut from the cob and cooked very briefly in a skillet.

Allow two ears or more per person and slice the kernels off with a sharp knife (you do not have to cut too deep). Then using the back side of the knife, scrape out the juice and pulp. Place corn, juice, and pulp in a large skillet and add a couple of tablespoons of butter, salt and pepper to taste, plus a tablespoon or two of milk. (If the corn is old you might want also to add a pinch of sugar.) Bring rapidly to a simmer, stirring all the while to prevent sticking. This will need only a few minutes of cooking time, depending on the age and type of corn you have.

If, by some miracle, there is any leftover, it may be added to salad or simply dressed with vinaigrette.

MELON WITH RED WINE GELATIN AND STRAWBERRIES

This red wine gelatin is good used with almost any combination of melon and berries. So use what is at hand if strawberries are not available.

1 envelope unflavored gelatin
2½ cups red wine
¾ cup sugar
One 2-inch cinnamon stick
1½ cups strawberries, hulled and cut in half
1 large melon, sliced and with the rind removed
Grated rind of ½ lemon (or more)

Garnish
Fresh mint

Sprinkle the gelatin over ½ cup of the wine. Set aside. Heat the rest of the wine and add the sugar and cinnamon stick. Bring to a boil, turn off the heat, and pour in the dissolved gelatin. Stir and let cool. Remove the cinnamon stick and refrigerate in a glass container. Just as the gelatin is about to set, stir in the strawberries, dispersing them evenly throughout.

To serve, give the mixture a stir to break it up (it should be like jellied madrilène) and serve over slices of chilled melon. Sprinkle with grated lemon rind and garnish with a sprig of mint.

Serves 6

The first thing to do when making this meal is put the gelatin together. It can take several hours to set (of course, you can do it the night before). The next thing is to get the salted cucumbers into the refrigerator. Then you can make the pasta cake. I think you should allow about 30 to 40 minutes of preparation time. And try to time yourself so that the cake can come out of the oven about when you want to eat. While the pasta is baking, slice the melon and grate the rind. Refrigerate. Assemble the salad at the last minute, while the cake is resting in its baking pan.

Nicolas Johns white-handled stainless steel flatware; Lee Bailey all-purpose bistro glass; Bennington Potters white spatterware plate; Frank McIntosh celadon linen napkin.

The Last Summer Lunch

O n chilly days, as the summer turns into fall, we continue to eat out on the deck by the water, sometimes even if to do so requires a sweater. It is our way of clinging to the season as long as we can.

Thinking back over some menus from past lunches, I realize that these cool-weather meals tend to have elements of both summer and fall in them, as if to bridge the seasons. The following is a good example: The soup that begins the meal is really something that would often be served in deep summer, because it looks so cooling. And the combination of uncooked cucumbers and tomatoes certainly reinforces the notion. However, it was chosen here for its very lightness, the chicken and warm potato salad that follows it being so hearty. Also, I especially like charcoaling in the fall, when the heat of the coals is welcome. And this chicken takes a minimum of time to finish, making cooking it a pleasure rather than a chore.

For dessert there is another reminder of summer, lime ice, and a cookie or two.

Above: *Lime ice and a crunchy cookie*
Left: *Charcoaled chicken breast garnished with endive and watercress with warm potato salad*
Far left: *Green soup topped with a dollop of sour cream and chopped chives*

MENU

Green Soup
Charcoaled Marinated Chicken Breasts
Warm Vinegar Potato Salad
Lime Ice
Cane Syrup and Walnut Cookies
Wine

GREEN SOUP

This soup has the texture of vichyssoise and also has potatoes as one of its principle ingredients. But, unlike vichyssoise, it has marvelous green-leaf vegetables in it. Best of all, it is made with no cream or milk. Guests are always surprised when I tell them this, because it has such a creamy texture. I serve it hot in the fall and winter and at room temperature during the warmer months.

- ¼ cup sliced green onions
- 5 tablespoons unsalted butter
- 2 cups diced raw potatoes
- 1 teaspoon salt
- 2 cups rich chicken stock
- 2 ounces arugula, stems removed
- 2 ounces spinach leaves, stems removed
- 4 ounces lettuce leaves
  Salt and white pepper to taste
  Sour cream or crème fraîche
  Chopped chives

Sauté the green onions in butter for 5 minutes, until wilted. Add the potatoes and salt and 1 cup of chicken stock. Simmer, covered, for 10 minutes. Tear the greens into small pieces and add. Simmer for another 10 minutes and test the potatoes for doneness. Purée the vegetables in a food processor; taste for seasoning, add the rest of the stock, and simmer for a minute or two.

Serve either hot or at room temperature, with a dab of sour cream or crème fraîche and a sprinkling of chopped chives on top.

Serves 6

CHARCOALED MARINATED CHICKEN BREASTS

Not only does this marinade give the chicken a zesty flavor, but the breasts require very little cooking time.

- 6 very small whole chicken breasts, boned, or 3 large, each cut in half
- 3 medium garlic cloves, crushed
- 1½ teaspoons salt
- ½ cup packed brown sugar
- 3 tablespoons grainy mustard
- ¼ cup cider vinegar
  Juice of 1 lime
  Juice of ½ large lemon
- 6 tablespoons olive oil
  Black pepper to taste

Garnish
  Endive leaves
  Watercress

Put the chicken breasts in a shallow bowl. Mix the garlic, salt, sugar, mustard, vinegar, and lime and lemon juices. Blend well. Whisk in the olive oil and add pepper. Pour over the chicken and refrigerate overnight, covered. Turn once.

Remove from the refrigerator an hour before you want to cook it and let come to room temperature.

Grill the breasts for approximately 4 minutes per side, or until done. Be careful not to overcook, as this will toughen them.

You may also do these under the broiler for the same amount of time.

Garnish with endive and watercress.

Serves 6

WARM VINEGAR POTATO SALAD

This has always been one of my favorite potato salads. I try to make it in batches just large enough for the meal, as I never like the flavor of it as well after it has been refrigerated. You might like a little more onion in it, and also adjust the amount of vinegar to suit yourself. It seems that on some occasions the amount called for in the recipe is fine but at other times it needs a bit more. Must have something to do with the type of potato used.

- 2 thick bacon slices, cut into small pieces
- 1 large onion, thinly sliced
- 2 tablespoons (¼ stick) unsalted butter
- 2 pounds potatoes, peeled and cut into cubes
- 1 teaspoon salt
- 1 cup hot chicken stock
- ¼ teaspoon black pepper
- ¼ cup apple cider vinegar

Using a very large skillet with a lid, fry the bacon until almost done. Add the onion and cook slowly until it is wilted and starting to turn color. Add the butter, and when it has melted spread the potatoes on top evenly. Sprinkle with salt and add the chicken stock. Bring to a boil, then turn the heat down to a simmer. Sprinkle on the pepper and cover. Cook, covered, for 20 minutes. Uncover and cook for 12 to 15 minutes more, shaking the pan occasionally. By the time you finish cooking this there should be almost no liquid in the pan.

Add the vinegar and carefully move the potatoes around to mix thoroughly but gently. Cover and let sit for 10 more minutes before serving.

Serves 6

LIME ICE

This makes a very tart ice, so if you have a sweet tooth, add more sugar.

1½ cups lime juice, fresh only
½ cup water
2¼ cups confectioners' sugar

Combine all the ingredients and mix well. Refrigerate for several hours, then freeze in an ice-cream freezer.

If you would like to do this in the freezer compartment of your refrigerator, put the mixture in metal ice-cube trays (without the dividers) and freeze, stirring every 20 to 30 minutes to keep it from freezing solid. Garnish with lime slices.

Makes a little less than a quart

CANE SYRUP AND WALNUT COOKIES

Somehow, thinking of cooler weather brings to mind a family recipe for cookies made with cane syrup. I think of them as being related to gingerbread, not being very sweet and having a nice soft texture. They would be good with the tart lime ice. Incidentally, if you don't know cane syrup, give it a try on your pancakes.

12 tablespoons (1½ sticks) unsalted
    butter, softened
1 egg
1 cup cane syrup
¼ cup hot water
1 teaspoon vanilla extract
3 cups flour
1 teaspoon baking soda
¾ teaspoon salt
1½ cups coarsely chopped walnuts

Preheat the oven to 325 degrees. Lightly grease a cookie sheet.

Mix together the butter and the egg. When blended, add the cane syrup, then the hot water and vanilla. Mix well and set aside for a minute while you combine the flour, baking soda, and salt. Stir the flour mixture into the other ingredients. Add the walnuts last.

Drop dough by the tablespoonful on the cookie sheet and bake for 15 minutes, or until the edges begin to turn slightly brown. Let cool on a rack.

Note: These cookies freeze well.

Makes approximately 3 dozen

GAME PLAN

To prepare this lunch you must start the evening before, because the chicken should have time to absorb the flavor of the marinade. Once that is done, you could also mix up the ice and set it aside in the refrigerator, ready to be frozen the next day.

A couple of hours before lunch, make the soup. I like it to be just warm, and if left on the back of the stove after it has been made it will stay at about the right temperature. (After it cools slightly, press a layer of plastic wrap directly onto the surface of the soup. This will keep a film from forming on it.) Although it has a potato base, green soup is not as good chilled as soups that contain cream, and I like this to be made with chicken stock and no cream.

The next thing to do is the ice. If you are not going to make it in an electric freezer but in the refrigerator freezer, start now, as it can take several hours to come to the right consistency.

After all this is finished (it won't take very long) you may either wait until almost lunch to get around to the other things or start on the potato salad by frying the bacon and sautéing the onion. The bacon-onion mixture can wait for several hours at this point, so all you will have to do later is add the potatoes and stock, which I would do about an hour before planning to start the chicken. (And speaking of chicken, take it out of the refrigerator now so it can warm up before you charcoal it.)

Finally, don't forget that it takes charcoal about 45 minutes to burn down enough to be right for cooking.

C'Ports stainless steel flatware; Pottery Barn wineglass; Bennington Potters black agate on slate spatterware plate; Bailey-Bannett Inc. glass bowl and stainless steel saucer (page 35); Frank McIntosh apricot linen napkin.

From the Raspberry Patch

Raspberries are terribly expensive, even in season—not because they are difficult to cultivate or require any special attention, but because they are so perishable and must be gathered by hand. However, anyone who has a spot of land in the full sun, away from the main part of his or her property, can grow them with ease. Since they are so hardy, they should be planted where they will not interfere with other plants. And since they are not really too ornamental, unless planted on frames, you don't want to have them where you will have to look at the vines. In common with most homegrown eatables, when their season hits you have more of them than you known what to do with—even raspberries. So if you grow this delicate little berry, and I hope you will, here are some things you might like to make with them.

Of course, raspberries are utilized in endless tarts and custards, but there are so many recipes around in that category that I wanted to give you some other simple ways of using raspberries.

Incidentally, I know that when someone suggests starting something like a patch of berry vines, most people are not inclined to follow through because they just assume it will take years for the vines to produce fruit in any quantity. This is certainly not so when it comes to raspberry vines. On the third summer after those in back of my garden were planted, I found myself trying to give berries away. So get to it. They like to be fed heavily with a good strong fertilizer at first and after that must have their old canes cut back, but otherwise can be left on their own. Mine are not even on frames—although, of course, that would make them more attractive, not to mention much easier to harvest.

RASPBERRY SHORTCAKE

I'm sure everyone has had that great American delight, strawberry shortcake. But for some reason, not many people serve raspberry shortcake—as obvious as it is. So here you have it, my favorite way, on a giant biscuit (which makes a spectacular presentation) instead of on cake. You could also serve this more conventionally, by making individual biscuits for each serving. These biscuits can be made in advance and reheated slightly, but since they take so little time to prepare, I'd make them fresh.

I seldom serve this for dessert after a meal. It is really almost too excessive following the usual country dinner. My favorite time to have it is in the late afternoon, as a surprise treat. Of course, everyone will dutifully talk about how they shouldn't be eating something so sinful in the middle of the afternoon. But they can always blame the host.

Sugar to taste
2 cups raspberries (or more)
2 cups flour
⅛ teaspoon salt
4 generous teaspoons baking powder
½ teaspoon cream of tartar
2 tablespoons sugar
½ cup safflower oil
⅔ cup milk
Whipped cream

Preheat the oven to 425 degrees. Grease a cookie sheet and very lightly dust it with flour. Set aside.

Sugar the raspberries to taste—about 6 tablespoons is average. Refrigerate, covered.

Mix the flour, salt, baking powder, cream of tartar, and sugar in a bowl. Make a well in the middle and add the oil. Mix and then cut in with a pastry blender or two knives until it resembles coarse meal. Add the milk all at once and stir. This should produce a very sticky mass; if it is not sticky, add just a little more milk. Pour and scrape out onto the cookie sheet. Jiggle it around until it makes a circle about 8 inches in diameter. Sprinkle this with a little extra sugar. Bake for 20 minutes, or until golden. This will be a large biscuit, brown around the edges. When cool enough to handle, slide it onto a serving plate. (Some people butter the top of it, but enough is enough.) Mound about two thirds of the berries in the center of the biscuit. Top with whipped cream and the rest of the berries. Cut in wedges to serve. Serve extra whipped cream (and more berries, if you have them) on the side.

Serves 6 to 8

CHICKEN WITH RASPBERRY VINEGAR

Here is a very easy recipe for making plain roast chicken more tasty by using some of your vinegar.

    4   tablespoons (½ stick) unsalted butter
    4   tablespoons safflower oil
   12   small chicken thighs
    2   whole chicken breasts, split in half
   ¾   cup finely chopped onion
    3   tablespoons finely chopped shallot
   ¾   cup Raspberry Vinegar (recipe follows)
  1½   tablespoons Italian tomato paste (or 1 small
          tomato, peeled, seeded, and chopped)
   ¾   cup chicken stock
    1   tablespoon chopped fresh parsley
   ½   cup crème fraîche
          Salt and pepper to taste

Garnish
    Fresh raspberries

Preheat the oven to 350 degrees.
    Heat 2 tablespoons of the butter and all the oil in a skillet large enough to hold all the chicken pieces. Carefully brown the pieces in two batches. Be careful not to burn them. When both batches are finished, fit the chicken pieces snugly in the pan. Lay a sheet of foil loosely over the top. Bake for just 1 hour.
    Remove the chicken and keep warm. Pour out the fat from the skillet, then add the remaining butter. Add the onion and shallot and sauté until wilted. Add the vinegar and cook at high heat until the mixture is reduced to a syrupy consistency. Dissolve the tomato paste in the chicken stock. Add this and the parsley to the vinegar mixture and simmer for a few minutes. (If using fresh tomatoes, instead of paste, reduce the mixture by cooking it very slowly for about 5 minutes.) Stir in the crème fraîche. Correct the seasoning with salt and pepper.
    Fit all the chicken pieces back into the pan and simmer for another few minutes, spooning the sauce over them continually or turning them several times.
    Serve garnished with fresh raspberries.

Serves 6

RASPBERRY VINEGAR

Fill with raspberries any kind of glass container that has a tight fitting top. Pour in enough apple cider vinegar to cover the berries and close the container. Set it in a spot where the sun will heat it every day.
    Let it mature for at least 8 days. Carefully pour off the vinegar through a fine cheesecloth and discard the berries.

RASPBERRY SYRUP

This syrup (like the vinegar above) has many uses. For instance, it is wonderful on pancakes or as a topping for custards and ice creams. And it takes only a few minutes to make—perfect for the times when you have gathered too many berries and don't quite know what to do with them.

    1   pint raspberries, washed
  1½   cups sugar
    2   teaspoons fresh lemon juice

Put the berries in a small enameled pan and top with the sugar. Place over low heat, stirring occasionally. When bubbly, cook for about 10 minutes. Add the lemon juice. Let cool slightly and put through a sieve. Discard the seeds. Pour into a container, cover tightly, and store in the refrigerator.

Makes approximately 2 cups

RASPBERRY ICE

Another way to use your raspberry syrup is to make raspberry ice, or granita. Simply measure out a quantity of syrup and then add one third the amount of water. Mix well and freeze it in an ice-cream freezer or in metal ice-cube trays (without the dividers) in your refrigerator freezer. Stir every 20 to 30 minutes until it sets. Break up any large pieces before serving. If it should freeze solid, break it all up and put in a food processor fitted with the steel blade. Give it a few quick whirls. Refrigerate to let it set again for a few minutes.

Endive salad with raspberry vinaigrette

Pork chop with raspberries

Raspberry fritters with raspberry syrup

Raspberry butter with biscuits

Raspberry shortcake

Raspberry vodka

RASPBERRY FRITTERS

These wonderful little fritters are perfect as a dessert or can be served for a special breakfast with good baked Canadian bacon, maple syrup, and Raspberry Syrup. Either way, they are worth the effort.

    1 cup lightly sugared raspberries
 1½ cups flour
    2 rounded teaspoons baking powder
 ½ teaspoon salt
    1 tablespoon sugar
    2 tablespoons (¼ stick) melted unsalted butter
    2 eggs, lightly beaten
      Milk
      Safflower oil for frying

Garnish

      Raspberry Syrup (page 41)
      Powdered sugar

Mix the dry ingredients in a bowl. Make a well in the middle and gradually pour in the butter and eggs. Blend well and add the milk, a few tablespoons at a time, stirring after each addition until smooth but not runny. You should be only just able to shake the batter from the spoon. This consistency is important.

Heat safflower oil in a deep pot (you should have at least 2 inches of oil) until very hot. Make fritters in a number of batches. You don't want to mix all the berries in at once, because that would break them up. Instead, mix a few tablespoons in at a time, and fry until dark golden. Be careful not to burn them, but the fritters must be cooked thoroughly. Drain on paper towels. Repeat until all the berries and batter are used up. (Any leftover batter can be fried and eaten plain with powdered sugar.)

Serve on a slick of raspberry syrup, sprinkled with powdered sugar.

Makes about 12

HONEY CUSTARD WITH RASPBERRY SYRUP

Here is a recipe for a plain custard that is transformed by just having a little of the fresh raspberry syrup poured over it.

    2 cups whole milk
    4 tablespoons honey
    3 eggs
      Pinch of salt
      Freshly grated nutmeg (optional)
      Raspberry Syrup (page 41)

Preheat the oven to 375 degrees. Put a kettle of water on to boil.

Scald the milk, being careful not to scorch it. Stir in the honey and set aside. Beat together the eggs and salt. Add a little of the milk mixture to the eggs and continue to stir. Add the rest of the milk mixture and mix well. Pour into 6 individual custard cups and set in a pan. Surround with boiling water and bake for 30 to 40 minutes, or until a knife inserted in the center of one comes out clean. Remove from the water and let cool. Sprinkle with nutmeg, if desired. Refrigerate. Serve with a generous slick of raspberry syrup on top of each and more on the side.

Serves 6

PORK CHOPS WITH RASPBERRY SAUCE

I like the flavor of something slightly sweet with pork, so raspberries come in handy for this delicious little sauce. As you can see, it is also another way to use some of your raspberry vinegar.

When I make chops this way I let them be the star of the meal, accompanied only by buttered pasta and followed by a watercress salad.

    6 thick pork chops, trimmed of fat (totaling approximately 3 pounds)
    5 tablespoons unsalted butter
    3 tablespoons safflower oil
      Salt and black pepper
      Flour for dredging
    3 medium onions, thinly sliced
    2 cups chicken stock
    1 tablespoon Raspberry Vinegar (page 41)
    1 generous cup fresh raspberries

Preheat the oven to 350 degrees.

Put 3 tablespoons butter and the safflower oil in a skillet large enough to hold the chops in one snug layer. Salt and pepper them and dredge on both sides with flour. Brown them in the butter and oil. Remove the chops and pour out the fat. Wipe out the skillet and cover the bottom with an even layer of sliced onions. Put the pork chops on top. Pour in enough stock to come up about ¼ inch. Cover and bake for 1 hour and 15 minutes. Check after about 45 minutes to make sure stock has not boiled away. The onions should get dark golden but not burn. Add more stock if necessary.

When done, remove the chops to a warm platter and degrease the pan with the 2 cups stock, simmering for a minute or two. Add the vinegar and whip in the 2 remaining tablespoons of butter. Add the berries and mash them gently. Reduce until slightly thickened. Correct the seasoning; you should not need to add more salt. Spoon the sauce over the chops as they are served, and garnish with a few fresh berries if you like.

Serves 6

RASPBERRY BUTTER

This butter is so good you could almost eat it just as it is. As a matter of fact, it would make a wonderful dessert served with cheese and thin rounds of crusty French bread. It is perfect on toast in the morning or on scones with afternoon tea. Speaking of tea, this butter is also good on the flat, slightly sweet little oatmeal biscuits that come from England and Scandinavia. They are a lighter snack than scones.

Raspberry butter will keep very well in the refrigerator, but never lasts very long once guests discover it.

 12 tablespoons (1½ sticks) unsalted butter, softened
  8 tablespoons Raspberry Syrup (page 41), simmer to reduce to 6 tablespoons
  ½ cup fresh raspberries

Put all the ingredients in a bowl and blend thoroughly with a hand mixer or wooden spoon. Smooth the mixture into a bowl and refrigerate, covered.

Makes approximately 1 cup

RASPBERRY VODKA

Fill a glass bottle about two thirds full with washed raspberries. Pour vodka over them, filling the bottle all the way. Cap it and refrigerate for several days before using (with soda or tonic water or anything else that suits you).

This can also be put in the freezer to be drunk neat, without a mixer. Not for the amateur.

ENDIVE SALAD WITH RASPBERRY VINAIGRETTE

Here your raspberry vinegar can be used yet again. Its flavor is marvelous with the slight bitterness of endive. And the salad itself is beautiful to look at.

Endive salad can be part of an elegant little summer lunch, served with sautéed slices of turkey breast. (See page 92.) In that case the turkey should have a good grind of black pepper over the top and be accompanied by lemon wedges. A good crusty bread with sweet butter would round the whole thing out, and you have a lunch that doesn't take too long to get on the table.

 6 large heads endive, leaves separated, washed and dried
 2 scraped carrots, cut into very thin strips with a stripper or large-gauge zester
 ¾ teaspoon salt
 ½ teaspoon black pepper
 2 tablespoons Raspberry Vinegar (page 41)
 6 tablespoons safflower oil
 3 tablespoons olive oil
 ¼ cup fresh raspberries

Arrange the endive leaves on individual salad plates and sprinkle carrot strips over the center of each. Make a vinaigrette of the salt, pepper, vinegar, and oils. Just before spooning it over the endive, mash in the raspberries. Grind more pepper over each salad if you like.

Serves 6

Eating
Outdoors

I think everyone in the country loves to eat outdoors. It must have something to do with some sort of sense memory of the time when eating outdoors was the only place we had to eat.

Certainly I remember vividly what a joy it was for me as a child to stand around a fire scorching my knees and hands while burning weenies and marshmallows. I surely ate as much charcoal as I did food, but no matter. It was bliss. And so it is today. I may have lost my taste for the crunch of charcoal over the years, but not my enthusiasm for eating in the open air.

When trying to figure out how to best organize this section, I decided that instead of making menus, it would be more helpful to group things by categories: sandwiches, meat pies, salads, cookies, and a couple of miscellaneous items that don't quite fit anyplace—giving you the option of putting them together in any fashion that suits you.

As is always the case, the recipes here are just a start on which to build. Cookies can go with ice cream if you are eating in your own backyard or with soft drinks if you are going on a proper picnic. Meat pies are for a picnic, but the sandwiches are for anywhere. Besides, these are not your usual sandwich. They are spreads to put on hearty bread once you get to where you are going—to be eaten along with green onions or radishes, or little cherry tomatoes (try the yellow ones if you see them). Later create your own spreads, using the ones here as a guide. And speaking of sandwiches, if it is convenient to do so, it is a good idea to take the ingredients in sealed containers and assemble them once you get there. Most sandwiches are better if they don't have to be made too far in advance, so the bread won't get soggy and the whole thing mashed around.

Always take along a little extra fruit and plenty to drink. Everyone is always thirsty outdoors. And don't forget the bottle opener and extra salt and pepper.

BLACK OLIVE TARTS

I am very partial to capers, but I find people to be about evenly divided between those who share my enthusiasm and those who don't. Their strong, distinctive flavor appeals to me, but they could be omitted here if you like.

Crust
- 1½ cups flour
- ½ teaspoon salt
- 4 tablespoons (½ stick) unsalted butter, frozen
- 6 tablespoons (¾ stick) margarine, frozen
- 5 to 6 tablespoons ice water

Filling
- ½ cup pitted Greek black olives in oil
- ½ cup pitted Italian black olives in oil
- 1 heaping teaspoon capers
- 5 tablespoons olive oil
- 3 tablespoons fresh lemon juice
- 6 heaping tablespoons finely chopped onion
- 3 medium garlic cloves, chopped
- 1 small tomato, peeled, seeded, and chopped

To make the crust, put all of the ingredients except the ice water in a food processor. Process until the mixture has the texture of small peas. Add the water and process until the mass begins to form a ball. Remove, shape into a ball and place between two pieces of waxed paper. Flatten slightly and refrigerate while you make the filling.

Preheat the oven to 350 degrees.

Chop the olives coarsely and add the capers, olive oil, and lemon juice. Put a few tablespoons of the oil from the olive mixture in a skillet and sauté the onion and garlic. Add the tomato and continue to cook for just a minute or two, to give any tomato liquid a chance to evaporate. Mix the tomato mixture in with the olive mixture.

Roll out the pastry and cut into 4- to 5-inch squares. Put 2 tablespoons of the filling in the center of each and dampen the edges of the square with a bit of the olive oil. Fold over to make a triangle. Seal the edges with the tines of a fork. Continue, rerolling the dough as necessary, until it is all used. Put the tarts on a greased cookie sheet and bake for 25 to 30 minutes. Let cool on a rack.

Makes approximately 8 tarts, depending on the size of the squares

SMOKED FISH SANDWICHES

You could use anything from smoked eel to smoked bluefish to make this spread. It has a marvelous flavor, and although it is not particularly perishable, I can guarantee it won't last long.

- 1 pound smoked whitefish
- 6 tablespoons sour cream
- 2 tablespoons fresh lime juice
- 1 tablespoon fresh lemon juice
- 4 drops Tabasco sauce
- Black pepper to taste

Skin and bone the fish, and discard the skin and bones. Put the flesh in a food processor along with all the remaining ingredients. Purée to a paste. Serve on dark bread with cherry tomatoes, lemon slices, and black pepper.

Makes approximately 2 cups

LAMB AND ZUCCHINI TART

Obviously, you may substitute another kind of meat for the lamb, but this way it's a change from all the meat pies based on beef or pork.

Crust (see page 48)

Filling
- 9 ounces ground lamb
- 2 tablespoons olive oil
- ½ medium zucchini, grated
- 5 large green onions (with some top), coarsely chopped
- 1 large garlic clove, finely chopped
- 2 teaspoons unsalted butter
- 1 tablespoon tomato paste dissolved in 1 teaspoon warm water
- ½ teaspoon salt
- ¼ teaspoon black pepper

Preheat the oven to 350 degrees.

Sauté the lamb in the olive oil until it turns color. Pour out the oil and reserve the meat. Sauté the zucchini, green onions, and garlic together in butter until the zucchini gives up its water and the vegetables are wilted but not browned. Add the meat, tomato paste, salt, and pepper. Simmer for just a minute.

Roll out the pastry and cut into 4- to 5-inch squares. Put 2 tablespoons of filling in a line down the middle. Dampen the edges of the square with water. Fold over to make a cigar shape and seal the three sides with the tines of a fork. Transfer to a greased cookie sheet and bake for 25 to 30 minutes.

Makes approximately 12 tarts

WHITE BEAN SANDWICHES

You could perk this up with any number of other ingredients, like chopped pine nuts or roasted peppers. Suit yourself.

This makes a fairly large quantity, so if you are not a sizable group, cut the whole thing in half.

- 1 pound small dried white beans
- ½ pound salt pork
- 2 bay leaves
- 2 garlic cloves
- 2 whole cloves
- ½ teaspoon dried thyme
- 2 tablespoons olive oil
- 1 tablespoon finely chopped fresh parsley
- 2 teaspoons fresh lemon juice
- ½ teaspoon black pepper
- ½ teaspoon salt
- 8 drops Tabasco sauce

Soak the beans overnight and drain. Pour on fresh water to come about 2 inches over them. Add the pork, bay leaves, garlic, cloves, and thyme. Simmer, skimming as needed, for 1½ hours, or until tender. Drain, reserving the liquid. Remove the bay leaves and the pork. Cut any lean meat from the pork, discarding the fat and rind. Put the pork in a food processor and chop coarsely. Then add the beans, along with the olive oil, parsley, lemon juice, pepper, salt, and Tabasco sauce. Purée. Correct the seasoning. To make sandwiches, spread on thickly sliced bread and top with watercress and green onions.

Store in the refrigerator with a lick of olive oil on top to keep it from drying out. You can make soup of of this by adding reserved bean liquid and chicken stock to the desired consistency.

Makes approximately 4 cups

HOT TURNIP RELISH

This is a condiment, not to be eaten by itself but as an accompaniment to another dish—fish, meat, or a meat sandwich.

- 2 cups finely shredded turnips
- ¾ cup finely grated white onion
- ½ cup rice wine vinegar
- 3 tablespoons prepared horseradish
- 3 tablespoons sugar
- ¾ teaspoon salt

Mix together all of the ingredients and refrigerate until ready to serve.

Makes approximately 3 cups

Above: *A basket of mixed meat pies.* Below left: *Hungarian cake.* Below right: *China tea eggs*

Below: *White bean spread*

Below: *Sausage and cheese drop biscuits*

Above: *Basket of mixed cookies.* Below: *Chocolate brownie pie*

CHICKEN, WALNUT, AND RED PEPPER TARTS

I don't think I would tamper too much with this one, except maybe for the nuts, which might be changed to pecans or hazelnuts. I like it pretty well as it is.

Crust (see page 48)

Filling
1 tablespoon unsalted butter
8 ounces coarsely ground chicken breast (uncooked)
1 tablespoon margarine
2 heaping tablespoons chopped onion
3 heaping tablespoons very finely chopped sweet red pepper
2 heaping tablespoons coarsely chopped walnuts

Preheat the oven to 350 degrees.

Melt the butter in a skillet and sauté the chicken just until it turns white. Remove from the pan and set aside. Add the margarine to the pan and sauté the onion and red pepper until soft. Add the chicken and walnuts. Cook for just a minute.

Roll out the dough and cut into 4- to 5-inch squares. Put 2 tablespoons of filling in the center of each square. Shape and seal in any of the three ways mentioned above.

Bake on a greased cookie sheet for 25 minutes.

Makes approximately 12 tarts

HAM AND FIG TARTS WITH CHEDDAR CRUST

I especially like figs and so I use them in many recipes. However, if they are not available, or if they are not one of your favorites, you could probably use any dried fruit. The Cheddar crust could be used for a number of other combinations. I've never tried it, but I bet it would make a wonderful apple tart.

Crust
1½ cups flour
½ teaspoon salt
5 tablespoons grated sharp Cheddar cheese
4 tablespoons butter, frozen
4 tablespoons margarine, frozen
4 to 5 tablespoons ice water

Filling
2 tablespoons finely diced onion
3 ounces mushrooms, cleaned and diced
1 tablespoon unsalted butter
1 tablespoon margarine
3 ounces ham, diced
4 medium dried figs, chopped
1 rounded tablespoon pine nuts
Dash of black pepper

To make the crust, put all the ingredients except the water in a food processor. Process until the mixture has the texture of small peas. Add the ice water and process until the mass begins to make a ball. Remove and form into a ball and place between two sheets of waxed paper. Flatten slightly and refrigerate while you make the filling.

Preheat the oven to 350 degrees.

Sauté the onion and mushrooms in the butter. Remove from the heat and add the remaining ingredients. Mix well.

Roll out the dough and cut into 4-inch squares. Place about 1½ tablespoons of the filling in the center of half the squares. Cover each with another square of dough. Using a round tart cutter, cut and seal each square. Continue, rerolling the dough as necessary, until it is all used.

Bake on a greased cookie sheet for 25 minutes.

Makes approximately 8 to 10 tarts

SAUSAGE AND CHEESE DROP BISCUITS

The flavor of these delicious little biscuits holds even when they are just warm—fine to take on a picnic.

I thought they might be the sort of thing that would freeze well, but although the flavor is passable when thawed, it is nothing to compare with the way they taste before being frozen. So freezing should be a last resort.

1½ cups flour
¾ teaspoon salt
1½ teaspoons baking powder
¼ teaspoon baking soda
4½ tablespoons unsalted butter
1 cup plus 2 tablespoons buttermilk
½ pound sharp Cheddar cheese, grated
¾ pound sausage meat

Preheat the oven to 425 degrees.

Mix all the dry ingredients and cut in the butter with a pastry blender or two knives. When the mixture has the texture of small peas, add the buttermilk and blend. Add the cheese and sausage meat, making sure they are dispersed throughout.

Drop large tablespoonfuls onto a greased cookie sheet. Bake for 18 to 20 minutes, until well browned.

Makes approximately 18 biscuits

OLIVE SALAD

Add cheese, French bread, and tomatoes to this and you would have a fine little lunch—and an easy one to pack up and take along.

This is the sort of thing that can rest for weeks in the refrigerator, getting better as the flavors meld together. I often make it just to have on hand for a quick lunch at home.

If you can't find jicama, you could substitute water chestnuts or celery. What you want is a little crunch.

- ¾ cup halved pitted small green olives
- ¾ cup coarsely chopped pitted Greek olives in oil
- 1 sweet red pepper, roasted (see page 121), peeled, and seeded, cut into strips
- 1 generous tablespoon capers
- ½ cup jicama, peeled and cut into small dice
- ¼ cup wine vinegar
- ¼ cup olive oil
  Salt and black pepper to taste

Garnish
- 1 small red onion, cut into thin rings and separated

Put the olives, red pepper, capers, and jicama in a bowl and toss. Whisk together the vinegar and oil. Pour over the other ingredients. Add salt and freshly ground pepper. Refrigerate. Garnish with onion rings.

Makes approximately 4 cups

LIMA BEAN AND CHEESE SALAD

I have never done it, but I don't see why you couldn't use dried limas for this salad. They would be more trouble, but might give the whole thing a different flavor.

- Two 10-ounce packages frozen lima beans
- 1 teaspoon salt
- ½ teaspoon black pepper
- 2 tablespoons balsamic vinegar
- 3 tablespoons safflower oil
- 3 tablespoons olive oil
- 1 generous teaspoon Dijon-style mustard
- 2 tablespoons chives
- 6 ounces sharp Cheddar cheese, cubed

Cook the beans according to the directions on the box and drain. Make a dressing of the salt, pepper, vinegar, oils, and mustard. Pour over the beans while they are still warm. Marinate, refrigerated, until you are ready to serve them. Remove from the refrigerator and toss in the chives and cheese.

Serves 8

MARINATED MUSHROOMS

These are a good accompaniment to almost any kind of sandwich. Take toothpicks along to stab them with.

- 1 pound small mushrooms, cleaned and thinly sliced
- 1 large carrot, coarsely shredded
- 2 bunches green onions (with some top), cut into rings
- 1 cup good-quality olive oil
- ¾ cup raspberry vinegar
- 1 teaspoon dry mustard
  Pinch of salt
- ¼ teaspoon black pepper

Combine the mushrooms, carrot, and green onions in a bowl. Whisk together the rest of the ingredients and pour over all. Toss and refrigerate.

Serves 6 to 8

CHINA TEA EGGS

These eggs have a rather surprising sweetish taste. They are almost like a dessert egg. Good with buttered whole wheat crackers.

- 12 hard-boiled eggs
- 2 heaping tablespoons dark tea leaves
  Rind of 1 orange
  One 8-inch cinnamon stick
- 6 whole allspice berries
- 12 whole cloves

As soon as the eggs are hard-boiled (about 10 minutes), run cold water over them and crack their shells all over, but do not peel. Put the eggs in a pan and cover with water to about ½ inch above them. Bring to a boil and add all the remaining ingredients. Simmer for an hour. Remove from the heat and let cool in the tea. When the eggs are cool enough to handle, peel them and return them to the tea. Let cool completely. Refrigerate in the liquid until ready to serve.

Makes 12 eggs

Brandied peaches

Olive salad

Pickled mushrooms,
lima bean salad, and
turnip relish

BRANDIED PEACHES

When peaches are in season I make a batch of these to serve with meats and meat pies. They can be canned, but I don't go through all of that.

    3 cups sugar
    3 cups water
    4 whole cloves
    4 whole allspice berries
       One 4-inch cinnamon stick
    3 pounds unblemished peaches, dipped in
       hot water and peeled
    4 tablespoons brandy

Put the sugar and water in a large kettle and bring to a boil. Add the cloves, allspice, and cinnamon. Simmer for 5 minutes. Carefully add the peaches. Simmer for 5 minutes, until tender. Remove the peaches to a large sterile jar with a snap lid. Pour in the cooking syrup and top with the brandy. When cool, snap shut and store in the refrigerator.
  Let it mature for a few days before serving.

Makes 2 quarts

VENETIAN COOKIES

The three cookie recipes that follow I found in a box of papers that had belonged to my mother. Since she was a noncook, I suppose they were just something she had collected from a friend, planning someday to get around to cooking. The "Venetian" cookies are very good with ice cream or iced tea. They are not very sweet, so if you like, increase the amount of sugar by half. Taste one after they are done, and if you want still more sweetness, roll them in additional powdered sugar while they are still hot.

    ½ pound (2 sticks) unsalted butter, softened
    ½ cup powdered sugar
    2 cups flour
    1½ teaspoons vanilla extract
    2 cups finely chopped walnuts

Preheat the oven to 300 degrees.
  Cream together the butter and sugar. Add the flour, a little at a time, then mix in the vanilla. Stir in the nuts. Make into balls and flatten slightly. Bake for 15 minutes. These do not brown.

Makes 30 cookies

BITTERSWEET COOKIES

The original recipe from which these are made calls for bittersweet chocolate chips. I couldn't find them in a supermarket. The best thing to do is buy bittersweet chocolate in a chunk and chop it up. Made with the usual chocolate chips, these taste like an early version of Toll House cookies.

    8 tablespoons (1 stick) unsalted butter, softened
    ½ cup firmly packed brown sugar
    ¼ cup granulated sugar
    1 egg
    ½ teaspoon vanilla extract
    1 cup chopped pecans
    1 cup flour
    1 teaspoon baking powder
       Pinch of salt
       One 6-ounce package bittersweet chocolate
       chips or 6 ounces bittersweet chocolate, broken
       into small pieces

Preheat the oven to 300 degrees.
  Sift together the flour, baking powder, and salt and set aside. Cream together the butter and sugars. Beat in the egg and then the vanilla. Add the flour, a little at a time, then stir in the chocolate chips. Drop by small spoonfuls onto a well-greased cookie sheet. Bake for 15 to 18 minutes, until the edges begin to brown. Let cool slightly. Remove the cookies with a spatula and let cool on a rack.

Makes 36 cookies

TEXAS COOKIES

Don't ask my why these are called Texas cookies. Maybe the person who gave my mother the recipe was from Texas.

    1 cup flour
    ½ teaspoon baking powder
    ½ teaspoon salt
    8 tablespoons (1 stick) unsalted butter, softened
    2 cups firmly packed brown sugar
    2 eggs
    1 teaspoon vanilla extract
    2 cups coarsely chopped pecans

Preheat the oven to 350 degrees.
  Sift together the flour, baking powder, and salt. Set aside. Cream together the butter and sugar and beat in the eggs, one at a time. Mix in the vanilla. Add

the flour, a little at a time. When well mixed, spread on a very well oiled jelly roll pan. Sprinkle the pecans over it and bake for about 25 minutes. Cut into squares when almost cool and remove the cookies with a spatula.

Makes 36 cookies

CHOCOLATE BROWNIE PIE

Like most healthy Americans, I like a chocolate fix now and again. However, I don't think I qualify as a "chocolate freak," as some of my friends call themselves. This pie is for chocolate freaks. Enjoy.

Someone who knows about such things told me after tasting this that it would be perfect with a glass of cold milk. I just have to take her word for that. I don't like milk that much. My loss.

Chocolate Pastry
- ¾ cup flour
- 3 tablespoons tightly packed light brown sugar
- 12 tablespoons (1½ sticks) butter, fronzen and cut into small pieces
- 1 ounce unsweetened chocolate, grated
- ¾ teaspoon vanilla extract
- 4½ teaspoons evaporated skim milk

Filling
- 3 ounces unsweetened chocolate
- 2 ounces semisweet chocolate
- 12 tablespoons (1½ sticks) unsalted butter, softened
- 1 cup plus 2 tablespoons sugar
- 2 eggs, lightly beaten
- 1½ teaspoons vanilla extract
- ½ cup coarsely chopped pecans
- ½ cup plus 1 tablespoon flour

Topping
- 1 cup light brown sugar
- 3 tablespoons heavy cream
- 2 tablespoons (¼ stick) unsalted butter
- 1 teaspoon instant dark coffee granules
- ½ cup powdered sugar

Preheat the oven to 350 degrees.

Put the flour, sugar, butter, and chocolate in a food processor and process to the texture of coarse meal. Mix the vanilla with the milk and add to the other mixture. Process just to combine. Press into the bottom and sides of a 9-inch pie pan. This is likely to be rather sticky, so flour your fingers if necessary. Set aside.

Melt the filling chocolate in the top of a double boiler. Add the butter by the tablespoon, mixing after each addition. Off the heat, add the sugar. Mix thoroughly. Add the beaten eggs, half at a time. Stir in the vanilla and nuts. Add the flour in small quantities, mixing after each addition. Pour into the pastry shell and bake for 30 minutes, or until a cake tester inserted in the center comes out clean. Let cool.

Put the light brown sugar, cream, and butter in a saucepan. Measure and sift the powdered sugar and have it ready. Bring the mixture in the saucepan to a boil and turn off the heat. Add the powdered coffee and powdered sugar. Beat with a whisk or hand mixer until smooth. Pour over the top of the pie. It will begin to set very quickly.

Makes one 9-inch pie

HUNGARIAN CAKE

After Country Weekends *came out, I received a letter from a lady named Gayle Gorman. She had very nice things to say about my book and included this recipe, which I tried and liked. Hungarian cake is as sweet as the Venetian cookies are not. It is also very moist and sticky. Don't take it along on a bumpy trip or where you don't have anyplace to wash your hands. Instead, it should be served from the pan—under an awning.*

- 2 cups sifted cake flour
- 2 teaspoons baking powder
- 1 teaspoon salt
- 1¼ cup sugar
- 8 tablespoons (1 stick) unsalted butter, softened
- ½ cup sour cream
- ½ cup buttermilk
- 1 teaspoon baking soda
  Juice of 1 large orange
- 1 cup powdered sugar

Preheat the oven to 350 degrees.

Sift together the flour, baking powder and salt. Set aside. Cream together the sugar and butter. Mix the sour cream and buttermilk. Add the baking soda. Add the flour to the sugar-butter mixture, alternating with the cream-buttermilk mixture, ending with the cream. Bake in a lightly greased and floured 9 × 15-inch pan for a half hour.

While still warm, pierce the top of the cake liberally with a toothpick. Mix the orange juice and powdered sugar together. Pour over the cake. Serve from the pan.

Makes one 9 × 15-inch cake

THE CITY

The City

Right after Labor Day, when it is near the date for me to start spending most of my time back in the city, I typically fall into a slightly peevish, foot-dragging pattern. It is then that I have to do something to force myself to stay in town for the weekends—to resist the comfortable familiarity of the country house. My city apartment always seems strange at first, and I notice that I tend to complain about it a lot. (I notice this because other people notice it too and tell me to give them a break.) Well, the truth is I can't remember where anything is after those months in the country, and I can't remember if what I am looking for is even in town at all. You can see my problem. This is compounded by a glance in the refrigerator, which more often than not reveals a great depressing assortment of half-used jars of mustards and opened jams that have started to crystallize around the top. Oils have gone rancid, and weevils generally have had a fine vacation in all the dry staples. I'm getting crabby just thinking about it. Luckily, I know what to do to put myself back on track: have a group of friends over for dinner. This makes me search out the things that have been eluding me and

makes me remember my routine. These dinners always start off slowly, but pick up steam before the evening is over. By dessert, conversation has normally turned enthusiastic as we begin to assess the crop of upcoming events and fall into an inevitable mood of anticipation. My high spirits tend to last right through Christmas—a season I still love. Even today traditional food has the power to suffuse me with a feeling of (stuffed) conviviality and good will, so I can be found going happily about my business at a time when some good friends droop from just the thought of the holidays. Things don't pall for me until the week between Christmas and New Year's. This is *really* a good time to entertain.

While we are on the subject of traditional food, if you have never had a bird with corn bread stuffing, you sure have a treat in store. It is my favorite (without sage). I start thinking about it around the beginning of November. Writing about that kind of food makes me remember a year when disaster struck: I went for what I assumed was to be my usual Thanksgiving dinner, only to discover that the hostess had decided it would be fun to have chili instead of the meal I had been dreaming of for days. My psyche was reeling for a week after—put to rights only by *two* dinners, including the beloved corn bread dressing, prepared by a concerned friend the following week. Extreme situations require extreme solutions.

Anyway, between Labor Day and the New Year's blahs there always seem to be plenty of excuses to cook and get together with friends. While it is marvelous fun to skim through the crop of new restaurants haughtily doing a trendy business each fall, finally nothing can compare with a few close friends or a larger group, to include new friends, gathered in the privacy and coziness of your own apartment.

It used to be that such meals went on until all hours, but now they usually are over by midnight, after starting at eight. Also, there is a fairly new factor these days—a kind of public late-night chic that has cropped up in the cities. Some guests want to look in on the scene before calling it a night. So all in all this sensible hour for the end to the dinner party works well for everyone.

The low point of the year is February. What a tough month. That is when I need diversion. If I don't have a winter excur-

sion to look forward to, I console myself with friends, food, and the fireplace—preferably all at once. Happily, it is the shortest month.

But then comes March. Slowdown time. Not much action on the entertaining front, unless it is for a birthday or to celebrate some accomplishment of a friend's. It is then that my thoughts turn to the wonderful bounty in store for me over the green months. Because I am genuinely interested in food, I find that looking forward to the pleasures of the summer sets me to note-taking about things I want to remember to try my hand at in the country kitchen. I keep an old file folder handy, and every time something new pops into my mind to investigate, or if something reminds me of a dish or an eating experience from the past, I file it away for later.

I know all this sounds as if I do nothing but concentrate on entertaining. Obviously that couldn't be so, but I learned long ago that one of the best therapies for the psychic demands of a busy and work-filled life is the relaxed company of friends. Enjoying food together seems to do more toward creating that nourishing mood of relaxation than anything else I know of.

Elegant Saturday-Night Dinner

Veal chops with blackberries, oven potatoes, and string beans

aturday night is still a special night to me. However, I have done a complete about-face so far as my entertaining habits are concerned. It seems to me that years ago we always went out to dinner on Saturday nights and then on to some crowded spot to see, or be part of, the late-night entertainment. Nowadays it practically takes dynamite to get me out of the house on Saturday evening. Instead, my idea of a perfect time is to spend it with a few friends, sharing a good meal and conversation.

The main course of this little dinner, veal chops with blackberries, combines two of my favorite foods. The berries give the sauce an interesting tang, and it can all simmer along in the oven while you are in the living room. Accompaniments are oven potatoes and string beans, tossed with jicama. All in all, a simple yet very pleasing menu. It is the sort that I would serve for a special evening—one to mark some occasion.

The dessert is light: stuffed peaches, which you might want to serve with a glass of champagne.

MENU

Veal Chops with Blackberries
Oven Potato Slices
String Beans with Jicama
Stuffed Peaches
Wine
Coffee

Stuffed peaches sprinkled with grated lemon rind

VEAL CHOPS WITH BLACKBERRIES

Veal chops are very expensive, but to make this you should get the best cut of meat. And since it is special (and expensive), you don't want to overwhelm the veal. Of course, chops can be broiled or baked, but they always need a little sauce of some sort.

Blackberries are hard to come by in the winter. And although they are sold frozen, you usually find them only in specialty markets. I get around this by freezing a few batches, which I pick myself, when they are in season. If you don't have access to wild berries, buy them when they are plentiful and put them in your freezer. Even then they are not cheap, but it takes only a cup for this recipe.

There are many simple ways to cook veal chops using the basic method in this recipe. You might experiment with different berries or even other kinds of fruit. You might also add a bit of cream to the sauce instead of stock (or in addition to the stock), at the end of the cooking time.

    1½ tablespoons unsalted butter
    1½ tablespoons safflower oil
        Flour
    Six 1-inch loin veal chops, trimmed
        Salt
        Black pepper
    5   large shallots, chopped
    2   small carrots, scraped and coarsely shredded
    ½   cup dry white wine
    1   cup chicken stock
    1   cup frozen blackberries

Preheat the oven to 325 degrees.

Put the butter and oil in a deep skillet or casserole (with a cover) large enough to hold all the chops in one layer. Turn on the heat under it, and while it is slowly heating, flour the chops on both sides and shake off the excess. Sprinkle with salt and pepper. Carefully brown the chops on both sides; do not let the butter burn. Transfer to a platter and set aside.

Put the shallots and carrots in the pan and sauté for a couple of minutes, until wilted. Add the wine and let it bubble up for a few minutes before adding the stock. When the stock is simmering, put in the chops and baste them before covering the pan.

Bake for 1 hour. Remove the chops to a heated platter and very quickly boil the liquid to reduce it slightly, adding the blackberries in the last few minutes. Correct the seasoning if necessary. Spoon the sauce over the chops and pass the extra sauce.

Serves 6

OVEN POTATO SLICES

This is an easy way to get crispy and perfectly cooked potato slices. Unfortunately, the timing on them is a little difficult to gauge. Sometimes they require a bit of extra cooking to get them lightly browned. So try to plan to have a 15-minute leeway in your timing. If you can't manage this, the potatoes will taste perfectly good even if they are not as brown as you might wish.

    5   unpeeled medium red potatoes (about 2 pounds,
        of more or less uniform size, if possible),
        washed and cut into ¼-inch slices
    3   to 4 tablespoons unsalted butter
        Kosher salt
        Black pepper
        Rosemary (optional)

Preheat the oven to 425 degrees.

Melt the butter and pour half of it into a large shallow baking pan, making sure it covers the entire bottom. Layer the potato slices in rows, with each slice slightly overlapping the next. Sprinkle with salt, pepper, and rosemary, if desired. Drizzle the remaining butter over all and bake, uncovered, for 45 minutes, or until the potatoes begin to crisp and turn golden.

Serves 6

STRING BEANS WITH JICAMA

String beans are old dependables. Unfortunately, in many restaurants today they seem to be served barely cooked, something I am not too keen on. I suppose some chefs prefer crunch to flavor.

This way of preparing string beans seems to be a good compromise—the beans can be steamed until they are tender (which I think improves their flavor) and the crunch is supplied by the jicama.

If you have not come across jicama, keep an eye out for it. It is a vegetable from Mexico that became popular in the West and has moved east in the last few years. It has a marvelous texture and a very pleasant taste. It is often served raw, cut into strips, as a crudité with dip in California—which is how and where I first encountered it. Jicama is very good that way.

    2½ pounds string beans, with stems and tips cut off
    1   cup finely diced and peeled jicama
    1   tablespoon unsalted butter
        Fresh lemon juice
        Salt to taste

Put the string beans in a steamer and cook them to the degree of tenderness you like. Test the beans with the tines of a fork, and when they start getting soft, add the jicama to warm it through.

To serve, toss beans and jicama with butter, a squeeze of lemon, and salt.

Serves 6

STUFFED PEACHES

Now that you can get good fruit during the winter, simple desserts utilizing their warm-weather flavor make an excellent way to finish a delicious meal. The fact that another kind of fruit is used in the sauce for the veal doesn't bother me in the least.

These peaches are best if they are not refrigerated after cooking.

6 large peaches, peeled and cut in half, with pits removed
2 tablespoons (¼ stick) unsalted butter, softened
1 tablespoon sugar
1 egg white
1 teaspoon fresh lemon juice
2 teaspoons brandy
4 ounces amaretti cookies, crushed

Garnish

Cream mixed with vanilla extract (optional)
Grated lemon rind

Preheat the oven to 350 degrees.

Lightly grease an ovenproof dish and put the peach halves in it, cut side up. Set aside.

Cream together the butter and sugar and then add the egg white (this will not mix completely, but no matter). Add the lemon juice and brandy. Mix well. Add the crushed cookies and combine. Mound a large dab of this mixture in each peach cavity. Bake, uncovered, for 20 minutes.

Serve warm, preferably on a slick of cream. Add a little vanilla to the cream if you like. Spoon pan juices on each serving and top with a sprinkling of grated lemon rind.

Serves 6

GAME PLAN

There really isn't too much you can do in advance when you make this dinner. That is why it is the sort of meal I cook on the weekend, when I have more free time.

Of course, you can trim the beans and put them in water to soak; same with the jicama.

You can slice the potatoes and cover them with water, too, and prepare the pan to cook them in.

Speaking of the potatoes, you almost need two ovens to do these and the chops with, since they must cook at extremely different temperatures. If you don't have that arrangement, it might be better to substitute potatoes cooked on top of the stove—for instance, the skillet potatoes from *Country Weekends*, still one of my favorite methods. Or you might make wonderful light mashed potatoes, which you could prepare while the veal is in the oven. They may be finished and left to stay warm over hot (not boiling) water.

Put the beans on after you have finished the mashed potatoes, if that is what you are serving. If you are doing the potatoes in the oven, start the beans during the last 15 minutes of the veal's cooking time. They can hold a little after they are cooked, or the veal can if it finishes first.

If you think it would make your life easier, cook the veal chops up to the point where you make the sauce (before adding the berries and reducing the pan juices) and let them stay in the warm essence of the pan. Then quickly warm them when you are about ready to serve and set them aside on a warm platter while finishing the sauce. Frankly, they will be slightly overcooked (the way almost all rewarmed food is, inevitably), but they will still be tasty. Dealer's choice.

David Mellor silverplate flatware; Williams-Sonoma wineglass; Villeroy & Boch flowered porcelain plate; D. F. Sanders pale pink napkin.

Winter Seafood Dinner

Cucumber,
walnut, and
endive salad

Because today's fish markets in the city offer so much prepared or partially prepared fish and seafood, seafood risotto, around which this menu is planned, becomes extremely easy. Before such conveniences existed, there was a fairly large amount of odorous preparation that had to be done to get the ingredients ready—boiling and cleaning lobsters and shrimp, as well as steaming clams. And, worst of all, making fish stock from fish heads.

Although preparing this risotto means you will have to spend about 30 minutes in the kitchen just before the meal is served, that isn't so bad when you consider what the preparation was in the past. Seafood risotto also has the advantage of making a comparatively little bit of expensive seafood go a long way.

As an accompaniment, I would opt for a salad after, unless you think serving another course would be too much bother. In that case, a combination of vegetables such as cauliflower and lima beans is nice.

For dessert, there is coffee flan.

MENU

Seafood Risotto
Cucumber, Walnut, and Endive Salad
with Walnut Vinaigrette
Crusty Bread and Sweet Butter
Coffee Flan
Wine
Coffee

SEAFOOD RISOTTO

Don't be dismayed or discouraged by the long list of ingredients. There are lots of them, but they are almost all in small quantities and are things you are likely to have on hand—except for the saffron, Arborio rice, and items you will be buying already cooked from your fish market.

 2 tablespoons (¼ stick) unsalted butter
 2 tablespoons margarine
 3 tablespoons olive oil
 1 large carrot, peeled and finely minced
 1 large rib of celery, finely minced
 1 medium to large onion, finely minced
 1 teaspoon fennel seed
 1 garlic clove, mashed
 1 cup chopped fresh parsley
 Approximately 1 quart fish stock, heated
 1½ cups Arborio rice (see Note, page 24)
 ¾ cup dry white wine

 ½ teaspoon saffron threads
 ½ cup hot water
 Black pepper to taste
 Salt (optional)
 ½ pound cooked shrimp, cut into large pieces
 12 steamed littleneck clams
 ½ pound cooked lobster (or crab meat), cut into large pieces

Garnish
 Lemon slices and parsley

In a large pot, melt the butter and margarine along with the olive oil. When it bubbles, add the carrot, celery, onion, and fennel seed. Sauté gently for about 10 minutes. Add the garlic and continue cooking for a minute, then add the parsley. Stir and cook for another minute or two.

Put on the fish stock to heat up.

Add the rice to the vegetables and stir until it is well coated. Cook, stirring, for several minutes, until the rice begins to turn white. Add the white wine and cook over medium heat until it has all been absorbed.

Begin adding the fish stock, just enough each time to barely cover the rice. Let it simmer, not boil. Stir occasionally to keep the rice from sticking to the bottom of the pot. It is better for it to cook too slowly than too fast. Continue this process until about three quarters of the stock is used. When rice starts to become al dente, dissolve the saffron in the hot water and add. Keep stirring. The rice is done when it is al dente, chewable without crunching. Add the pepper and salt. Sometimes fish stock is very salty, making additional salting unnecessary.

Quickly sauté the cut-up lobster and shrimp in a little additional butter and then carefully mix it in with the rice, using a fork. A couple of the steamed clams in their opened shells should be put on each individual plate. Garnish with lemon slices and parsley.

This ought to be eaten *without* Parmesan cheese and while it is hot.

Serves 6

CUCUMBER, WALNUT, AND ENDIVE SALAD WITH WALNUT VINAIGRETTE

The combination of cucumbers, walnuts, and endive is a surprisingly satisfying mix of flavors that you might not think would work together—but it is delicious. Dressed with a walnut vinaigrette and arranged on individual plates, it also makes a very appealing presentation.

Walnut Vinaigrette

- ½ teaspoon salt
- ¼ teaspoon black pepper
- 1 teaspoon Dijon mustard
- 2 tablespoons wine vinegar
- 2 tablespoons safflower oil
- 3 tablespoons walnut oil

- 1 small cucumber, peeled, seeded, and diced
- ¾ cup walnuts, coarsely chopped
- 6 medium endives, leaves washed and separated

To make the vinaigrette, put the salt, pepper, mustard, and vinegar in a small bowl and mix. Whisk in the oils and set aside.

Combine the cucumbers and walnuts. Arrange the endive leaves on individual plates and heap the cucumber mixture over them. Spoon the vinaigrette over all.

Serves 6

COFFEE FLAN

I like the coffee flavor of this and always enjoy the wonderful smooth texture of flan. If it is the right time of the year, berries are a welcome addition to this dessert.

- ¾ cup sugar
- 2 tablespoons water
- 2 cups whole milk
- 1 cup heavy cream
- 4 eggs plus 1 yolk, at room temperature
- 1 tablespoon powdered espresso coffee

Preheat the oven to 300 degrees and put a kettle of water on to boil.

Put ½ cup of the sugar in a small saucepan, along with the water. Have a 6-quart metal mold ready, as well as a potholder. Bring the sugar-water mixture to a boil and cook until it begins to caramelize. When it starts to change color it will go quickly, so be careful not to burn it.

When the sugar is a dark golden color, pour it into the mold. Tilt the mold around to coat the sides and bottom. This is where you will need the potholder, as the metal pan will heat up, making it very difficult to handle. Set aside.

Mix together the milk and cream in a saucepan and put on to scald. While this is heating, beat the eggs and yolk lightly and add the remaining ¼ cup of sugar. When the milk is scalded, pour a few tablespoonfuls into the egg mixture and stir. Then pour in the rest of the milk. Mix well. Add the powdered coffee and mix.

Strain the mixture into the mold and set in another, larger, ovenproof pan. Place a lid or ovenproof plate over the top of the mold and put the mold on the lower shelf of the oven. Surround it with boiling water and bake for 50 minutes.

To test for doneness, insert a metal knife. If it comes out clean, the flan is ready. Let cool and then refrigerate it.

To unmold, place the serving plate (which should have a slight lip) over the top and invert. Care must be taken here, as there is liquid around the flan, which you don't want to spill.

Serves 6 to 8

GAME PLAN

To prepare this dinner you first make the dessert and have it cooling in the refrigerator, unmolded and covered lightly with a piece of foil.

Arrange the endive on the individual plates and put them in the refrigerator if you have room. Lay paper towels on top. If there is no room, wash and separate the endives. Stow in a plastic bag and put the plates in to chill. Chop the walnuts and dice the cucumber, to be combined later. Refrigerate the cucumber with the endive. Make the dressing and leave it at room temperature.

Prepare all the vegetables for the risotto and set them aside until you are ready to start the dish.

Get back into the kitchen about 45 minutes before you want to serve. Have all your ingredients organized for the risotto and begin.

Serve the risotto on warmed plates, if you can manage it.

D. F. Sanders gray-handled stainless steel flatware, matte black plate, and gray and natural rough linen napkin; Progetti wineglass.

Dinner for a Frosty Evening

Peas, sausage, and fish with rice and zucchini

This menu is built around a stick-to-the ribs kind of dish that includes black-eyed peas, sausage, and fish. The combination may sound a bit odd, but the ingredients work very well together. It is served with rice that has been tossed with toasted coconut, for extra crunch and flavor, and with broiled zucchini. You could substitute a green salad for the zucchini if you would rather have one. Either would be fine.

The dessert is a sweet lasagna with vanilla sauce, an interesting concoction that is similar to one traditionally served in northern Italy around Christmastime.

The meal needs to be followed by cups of strong coffee before you send everyone off into the cold.

MENU

Black-eyed Peas, Sausage, and Monkfish
Rice with Toasted Coconut
Broiled Zucchini
Fruit Lasagna with Vanilla Sauce
Wine
Coffee

The main course ready for serving

Fruit lasagna garnished with lemon peel

BLACK-EYED PEAS, SAUSAGE, AND MONKFISH

Monkfish, called for in this dish, has a texture similar to lobster meat and is much cheaper. However, if you would like to substitute lobster for the fish, do so. Shrimp would do, too—or a combination of both. Should you elect to make this substitution, sauté the seafood in a little butter before adding it to the pot.

I wish more people would think of black-eyed peas as a winter dish. They are very healthful, have a marvelous flavor, and are extremely easy to prepare. Give these a taste after they have been cooked, before you combine them with the other ingredients. You will see what I mean. They are not just for good luck on New Year's Eve.

- 1½ cups dried black-eyed peas, soaked overnight and drained
  Chicken stock
- 1 pound hot Italian sausages, cut into 12 pieces
- 1 very large garlic clove, minced
- ¼ cup red wine
- 1 pound monkfish, cut crosswise into ½-inch slices
  Soy sauce
  Fresh lemon juice
- 3 tablespoons unsalted butter
- 2 tablespoons finely chopped fresh parsley
- 1 very large sweet red pepper, seeded and cut into strips
- 1 very large green pepper, seeded and cut into strips

Preheat the oven to 450 degrees.

Put the beans in a small pot and cover with chicken stock to about an inch above the beans. Simmer for approximately 30 minutes, or until they begin to get tender. When cooked, set aside.

Put the sausages in a cold large skillet and cook for 5 minutes before adding the garlic. Continue to cook until the sausages begin to brown. Add the wine and simmer, covered, for 15 minutes.

While this is cooking, rub the monkfish slices on all sides with soy sauce and place them in a single layer in a foil-lined pan. Squeeze lemon juice over all. Bake in the oven for 7 minutes. When done, set aside in the pan.

Add the butter to the sausages and when it melts add the parsley and peppers. Toss to coat with butter and cover. Cook for 4 minutes, or until the peppers begin to get tender.

To assemble, drain the cooked beans (reserving the liquid) and add them to the sausage-pepper mixture. Then add 2 tablespoons of the liquid from the fish pan and ¼ cup reserved bean liquid. Mix and simmer for 5 minutes, covered. Last, cut each slice of fish in half and toss very carefully with the other ingredients. Cover and simmer for just 2 or 3 minutes, to be sure the fish is heated through. Correct the seasoning if necessary.

Serves 6

RICE WITH TOASTED COCONUT

I have always been partial to the flavor of toasted coconut. It is not only good as it is utilized here, but also very nice sprinkled on vanilla cake icing while the icing is still damp (so it will adhere).

Grated coconut freezes quite successfully.

- 1 cup raw rice
- 2 tablespoons (¼ stick) unsalted butter
- 1 cup unsweetened grated coconut, toasted until golden

Put the rice in a saucepan and cover with salted water to an inch above the rice. Simmer, uncovered, for 10 minutes. Test for doneness. If not quite done, give it another minute or two. Drain and rinse with hot water. Put the butter in the hot saucepan and then return the rice to the pan. Mix, add the coconut, and toss. Correct the seasoning if necessary.

Serves 6

BROILED ZUCCHINI

The cooking time of these will vary slightly according to the size of the vegetable and how mature it is. Just test it with the tines of a fork. You may also sprinkle almost any herb you particularly like on the zucchini before broiling it. However, the main dish is rather spicy, so I opted for only butter, salt, and a grind of pepper.

- 6 small zucchini, cut in half lengthwise
- 2 tablespoons (¼ stick) unsalted butter, melted
  Salt and black pepper to taste

Preheat the broiler.

Place the zucchini halves on a lightly greased pan, skin side down. Score the flesh with the point of a knife. Drizzle the butter over all and sprinkle with salt and pepper.

Put under the broiler and cook for 5 minutes, until tender.

Serves 6

FRUIT LASAGNA WITH VANILLA SAUCE

Fruit lasagna reminds me of that marvelous sweet Jewish dish, noodle pudding. This is rather rich, so I would not make the individual servings too large. If you have any of this dessert left over, it should be refrigerated, but let it come back to room temperature before you serve it the second time around. Also, if the top layer of noodles has become tough from being refrigerated, remove and discard it.

The vanilla sauce is a very basic kind of sweet sauce. Although I like the flavor of liquor in it, you could add orange juice and more lemon rind in place of the rum.

    4   Granny Smith apples, peeled, cored, and
        coarsely grated
    2   teaspoons fresh lemon juice
    4   ounces dried figs, finely diced
    4   ounces dried dates, finely diced
    ½   cup golden raisins
    4   ounces coarsely chopped mixed walnuts
        and pecans
    ½   cup tightly packed brown sugar
    ½   pound lasagna noodles
    6   tablespoons (¾ stick) unsalted butter, melted
    2   tablespoons granulated sugar

Vanilla Sauce

    ⅓   cup sugar
    1   tablespoon cornstarch
    ¾   cup water
    2   tablespoons (¼ stick) unsalted butter
    1½ teaspoons grated lemon rind
    2   tablespoons vanilla extract
    2   tablespoons rum

Garnish

    Thin strips of lemon rind

Preheat the oven to 375 degrees.

Mix the apples, lemon juice, figs, raisins, nuts, dates, and brown sugar. Set aside.

Cook the lasagna noodles according to the directions on the box. Drain and cover with cold water to stop the cooking. Drain again and dry the noodles on paper towels.

Lightly butter a 10 × 12-inch pan and layer the strips of lasagna with the apple mixture, adding a bit of the melted butter on each layer. Finish with a layer of noodles and then pour the rest of the butter over it and sprinkle with granulated sugar. Bake for 40 minutes.

Meanwhile, combine the sugar and cornstarch in the top of a double boiler. Add the water and mix.

Cook over hot water until the mixture begins to thicken, then add the rest of the ingredients. Cook for several minutes more, until the mixture thickens again.

Top with Vanilla Sauce and a sprinkle of lemon rind.

Serves 12

GAME PLAN

If you forget to soak the black-eyed peas overnight, don't despair. Cover them with water and bring to a boil. Continue simmering for several minutes before turning off the flame. After an hour, pour off the water and go on with the recipe. Incidentally, this same quick-soaking method may be used for almost any variety of dried beans or peas in place of the usual overnight soaking.

You may make the main dish up to the point where you will be adding the fish and then put it aside. Finish it while the rice is cooking.

Next, make the lasagna and vanilla sauce. This is good warm, but if you can't swing that, serve it at room temperature.

Toast the coconut now, by putting it on a cookie sheet in a 350-degree oven. This will take about 15 minutes to turn golden brown. It will not have to be refrigerated.

After you have done all of this, you will then only have to cook the rice and fish, which take 10 and 7 minutes, respectively. While they are cooking, get the zucchini ready (the broiler will be heating and just needs to be turned up after you take the fish out of the oven) and broil it after everything else is ready. Luckily, the main dish can wait for a few minutes and the rice can stay warm over hot water.

All in all, a very easy dinner to organize.

Christofle silverplate flatware; Richard Meier for Swid Powell wineglass; Limoges celadon porcelain plate; D. F. Sanders dark gray linen napkin.

*The traditional
New Orleans "eye-
opener"—an Ojen
cocktail*

Eggs in brown butter

Festive Breakfast

MENU

Ojen Cocktail
Eggs in Brown Butter
Chili Sausage
Toast with Apricot Butter
Café au Lait

Café au lait

*Chili sausage
and toast
with apricot butter*

This is not only a special breakfast, but one that I would not attempt for more than a few friends at a time—not because it is so difficult to prepare or organize, but because it must be served hot, and the eggs must be cooked in batches.

Accompanying the eggs is a hot chili sausage—easy to make, but an element of the menu that you could buy ready-made if sausage making doesn't seem worth the effort. The flavor of sausage patties (which I prefer to links) varies greatly from source to source, so if you are going to buy them, try sausage from several places to find the right brand.

Apricot butter is another thing on the menu that you might change (to plain butter and apricot jam) if time is important, although it, too, is very easy to prepare.

I have suggested these variations of the familiar breakfast fare to give you a bit of variety and therefore make the occasion more festive. Suit yourself.

There is also a late-morning drink to serve your guests. Such "eye-openers" are usual in New Orleans, where this cocktail is popular. It is the sort of drink that I don't think you would particularly want to have more than one of, so it is not too indecent at 11:00 A.M.

OJEN COCKTAIL

Ojen (pronounced O-hen) is an absinthe substitute that is ubiquitous in New Orleans as a late-morning drink—before the late breakfast. As a matter of fact, I have never had Ojen any other place but in New Orleans. I think you will like its licorice flavor. If you cannot find Ojen, use Pernod.

  1½ ounces Ojen, or Pernod
  2 dashes of bitters
     Club soda

Fill a glass with crushed ice. Mix the Ojen and bitters with just a splash of club soda. Pour over the ice.

Makes 1 cocktail

EGGS IN BROWN BUTTER

My friend Diane Judge taught me how to make these eggs. She says the recipe came to her from her Dutch grandmother. It is truly a treat, and one of my favorite ways of eating eggs.

This recipe allows one egg per guest. If this is not enough, you might want to double it. If so, cook the eggs in two large batches (or even three) and keep them on a warm plate in a warm oven until all are done. Have everyone ready at the table as you finish frying.

  6 tablespoons (¾ stick) butter
  4½ teaspoons apple cider vinegar
  6 eggs
     Chopped chives
     Salt and pepper to taste

Brown half the butter in a small pan and add the vinegar, which will slightly boil away. Set aside to keep warm.

In a skillet large enough to fry three eggs comfortably, melt half of the remaining butter. Cook the eggs to the desired degree of doneness and put one on each warm plate. Repeat with the remaining butter and eggs. Pour the browned butter over each egg and top with chopped chives.

You may also bake the eggs in individual ramekins. In that case, pour the browned butter with vinegar over them and add the chives after they are cooked.

Serves 6

CHILI SAUSAGE

Chili sausage is hot and spicy—and very simple to make. You learn about sausage seasoning only by doing it, so try it this way the first time. Then add more or less of the ingredients to suit your own taste next time.

The sausage mixture should be made a day or two in advance and refrigerated so the flavors have a chance to mature before it is used.

I know this looks like an awful lot of ingredients, but don't let that stop you. Most sausage recipes call for a little bit of a lot of things to give it flavor.

  1 onion (about 3 ounces) coarsely chopped
  1 small garlic clove, cut into several pieces
  1 bay leaf, crumbled
  1 pound lean pork
  ½ pound pork fat
  ½ teaspoon salt
  ½ teaspoon black pepper
  ¼ teaspoon cumin
  ¼ teaspoon oregano
  ¼ teaspoon cayenne pepper
  ¼ teaspoon thyme
  ¼ teaspoon allspice
  ¼ teaspoon fennel seed

Tear off an 18-inch piece of waxed paper and another of foil. Set aside. Put the onion, garlic, and bay leaf in a food processor and purée. Scrape down the sides a time or two. Add the pork and pork fat and grind it with an off-and-on motion for just a second or two. Do not overprocess. Add all the remaining ingredients and process to about the texture of ground hamburger. This will make a very sticky mass because of all the pork fat.

Pour and scrape the sausage meat out onto the waxed paper and pat into a long French bread shape. When it is the right shape, roll it onto the foil and then roll the foil around it. Refrigerate.

To cook, cut off rounds (this will still be a bit sticky) about ¾ inch thick, put them in a cold skillet, and cook over medium to low heat until well done, flattening them slightly during the cooking prcess. They will give up a great deal of fat. Do not cook them too fast, or they will burn on the outside without cooking properly in the middle (remember that pork should never be pink in the middle). Drain them on paper towels.

Makes approximately 20 small patties

APRICOT BUTTER

Apricot butter has a very subtle aftertaste of fruit and is slightly sweet. Because you are adding so much to the butter, it does not get hard as regular butter would, which makes it easy to spread.

There is also a recipe for raspberry butter to be found on page 45.

- ½ pound (2 sticks) unsalted butter, softened
- 2 medium apricots, or 1 large peach (approximately 6 ounces), peeled, pitted, and cut into quarters
- 2 very generous tablespoons apricot jam

Put all the ingredients in a food processor and process until smooth. Scrape into a container and store, covered, in the refrigerator.

Makes about 2 cups

CAFÉ AU LAIT

This café au lait is simply strong coffee combined with caramelized sugar and warm milk. The caramelized sugar is a little twist our cook added when she made it for me as a child. I don't know if it is something she thought of or if it is usual in some parts of the country. Whatever, I grew up on café au lait and still love it. Of course, when I was young it was mostly milk, getting stronger and coffee-er as I got older.

After you have made a pot of good strong coffee, scald several cups of milk and set aside. Put 2 tablespoons sugar in a pot and melt it over medium heat. When it turns golden, add the hot milk and stir until mixed. Pour in the coffee to taste. Guests may add more sugar, coffee, or warm milk if they like.

GAME PLAN

Obviously, the sausage for this meal must be made a day or so in advance, to let it mature before you use it. However, the apricot butter is better if it is made and served right away.

So start getting this breakfast under way after you have given everyone a drink—because they are probably not going to have more than one.

Begin by cooking the sausage, which won't take too long. It can stay in the warm oven while you make the café au lait. This, too, can stand a slight wait, and even be rewarmed if it hasn't gotten too cold.

Have everything ready for the eggs before you start them. And I would ask one of the guests to make the toast while this is going on. Certainly, out of five guests one can be pressed into service. As I said earlier, get everyone to the table when you finish the first batch of eggs and you will be right on schedule.

Christofle silverplate flatware; Williams-Sonoma goblet; Baccarat porcelain plate; Frank McIntosh pink linen napkin.

Veal shanks with green pea salad

Onion bread pudding

Green pea salad

Date tart with cream

Make-Ahead Dinner

W hen I am very busy in the winter, but still would like to have a few people in to dinner during the week, I try to devise menus which allow me to cook the food over several days or at odd times. This one is typical. The veal shanks hold up very well when made ahead. As a matter of fact, I am not at all certain that the flavor isn't somewhat improved for having been made the day before. The same might be said for the date tart, which I always make in advance. However, the tart is the one thing on this menu that you could buy ready-made if you are just too pressed for time. The same old caution applies here as it does to buying all ready-mades: Never serve guests anything store-bought that you have not previously tasted.

This leaves the green pea salad, which may be made about five o'clock on the day of the party, and the onion bread pudding, which must be served hot but is extremely easy to prepare.

MENU

Country Veal Shanks
Onion Bread Pudding
Green Pea Salad
Date Tart
Wine
Coffee

COUNTRY VEAL SHANKS

This is my Cajun version of osso buco. I call it that because almost all Cajun meat dishes start with onions, sweet peppers (either red or green), garlic, and celery. I veer off by adding wine, chicken stock, and thyme, but the typical flavor is established by the vegetables.

It takes two veal shanks to get enough meaty slices for this dish. There is too little meat on the lower part of the shank to use as slices. After being browned like the others, these mostly bone pieces can be placed on top of the lower layer, to be cooked for another little meal.

Since you will likely be making this a day in advance, to reheat it put the veal in a very low oven (200 degrees) for about 30 minutes to warm it through. Then, right before serving turn the heat up to 350 degrees for about 20 minutes.

- 6 tablespoons (¾ stick) unsalted butter
- 6 tablespoons safflower oil
  Flour
  Six 1½-inch slices of veal shank, tied
- 1 medium to large onion, coarsely chopped
- 1 large sweet red pepper, coarsely chopped
- 1 large celery stalk, coarsely chopped
- 1 medium carrot, scraped and coarsely chopped
- 1½ cups dry white wine
- 1 cup chicken stock
- 1 large garlic clove, crushed
- ¾ teaspoon dried thyme
- ½ teaspoon salt
- ¼ teaspoon pepper

Melt 3 tablespoons each of the butter and oil in a heavy casserole or deep skillet with a lid. Lightly flour both ends of the tied veal slices and brown them in the hot butter and oil. Do not turn the heat up so high as to burn the butter. Set the meat aside, and if the butter has darkened too much, pour it out and wipe out the skillet. Add the remaining butter and oil. When hot, add all the vegetables and cook for 10 minutes, until wilted but not browned. Add the wine and simmer for another 20 minutes.

Meanwhile, reduce the chicken stock to ½ cup. Add it and the remaining ingredients to the vegetables.

Last, place the meat in a single layer on top and cover tightly. Simmer for 45 minutes, turn, and cook for another 30 minutes, covered. Remove the veal to a warm platter. Strain out the vegetables and put them through a ricer or purée in a food processor. Return the liquid to the pan and boil briskly to reduce slightly. To serve, spoon some sauce over each serving of meat and pass the rest.

Serves 6

ONION BREAD PUDDING

Onion bread pudding has a nice mild flavor to complement the meat. It shouldn't be made so far in advance that it will have to sit long, as it gets watery around the edges—which doesn't affect its flavor, just its appearance.

The one part of the recipe you could do in advance is chopping and sautéing the onions; they could sit for several hours that way. If you do this, reheat them slowly and go on to the next step.

If you are too rushed, you might substitute rice simmered in chicken stock, buttered, and sprinkled with a little finely chopped parsley for this recipe.

- 6 tablespoons (¾ stick) unsalted butter
- 3 cups coarsely chopped onion
- 4 cups milk
- 5 eggs, lightly beaten
- 2 teaspoons Worcestershire Sauce
- 1½ teaspoons salt
- ½ teaspoon black pepper
  Several dashes of Tabasco sauce
- 4 thin slices white bread, crusts trimmed and cut into quarters

Preheat the oven to 325 degrees. Put a kettle of water on to heat.

Melt half of the butter and add the onion. Stir to coat. Cover and cook very slowly for 10 minutes. Do not let it brown. While the onion is wilting, mix all the remaining ingredients (including the rest of the butter, melted) except the bread. Lightly butter a 2-quart casserole and put in the onion. Pour in the milk-egg mixture. Stir lightly to mix. Place the bread squares on top, cutting smaller pieces to fill in. Bake for 45 minutes to 1 hour, surrounded by hot water. To test for doneness, insert a knife in the center. It is done when the knife comes out clean.

Let it set for a few minutes before serving.

Serves 6 to 8

GREEN PEA SALAD

You might add other ingredients to this, such as finely chopped celery, but I really prefer it as it is. If you are especially fond of dill, the amount in the dressing might not be enough for you.

The peas hardly have to be cooked at all, if they are frozen. And if it is winter, frozen ones are as good as any so-called fresh ones you will come across. The peas should be carefully drained and cooled before they are mixed with the dressing. If not, the whole thing will get watery.

Two 10-ounce boxes frozen green peas,
 steamed until just tender (do not overcook)
3 tablespoons chopped fresh dill
2 tablespoons sour cream
2 tablespoons mayonnaise
2½ teaspoons fresh lemon juice
4 teaspoons olive oil
1 teaspoon Dijon mustard
½ teaspoon salt
¼ teaspoon black pepper
 Few drops Tabasco sauce

Garnish
 Dill sprigs

Mix the peas and dill and set aside. Whisk together all
the remaining ingredients. Add about three quarters of
the dressing to peas and toss lightly. Cover and refrigerate. To serve, correct the seasoning and mix in the
rest of the dressing. This may be made several hours
in advance. Garnish with a sprig of fresh dill.

Serves 6

DATE TART

*The recipe for this very easy tart was given to me by my
Aunt Freddie. It is a rich and dense dessert that needs
cream to balance it. You can make it as a pie, or in a
proper tart pan. If it is made in a pie pan, you may have
a little difficulty getting the first piece out, but after that
it will be all right.*

3 eggs, separated
¾ cup sugar
2 tablespoons flour
 One 10-ounce package pitted dates, coarsely
 chopped
1 cup coarsely chopped pecans
 Whipped cream or heavy cream

Preheat the oven to 325 degrees.
 Beat the egg yolks well and gradually add the sugar. Continue beating until lemon yellow. Combine the
flour with the chopped dates and pecans and add to the
egg yolk mixture. Mix well.
 In a separate bowl, whisk the egg whites until
they stand in stiff peaks. Dump them on top of the other mixture and fold in with an over-and-under motion.
 Pour into a well-greased floured pan. Bake for 45
minutes.
 Let cool before serving topped with cream,
whipped or not.

Serves 6 to 8

As I said in the introduction, the veal shanks will
probably be better if the dish is made a day or
even two in advance. When you do this, allow it to
cool completely before refrigerating it—always
tightly covered.
 If you can, make the tart at the same time.
Since it has no crust, it really doesn't require much
doing to finish. However, if you are going to serve
whipped cream with it, this is better done an hour
or so before you plan to eat dessert, not now. If
whipped cream has been refrigerated in the meantime, give it a stir, as it tends to separate.
 When I am serving plain heavy cream instead
of whipped cream, I still whip it slightly to give it
more body. You may flavor either one with vanilla
or whip in some grated lemon rind.
 The green pea salad tastes best if made a
couple of hours before serving. However, you
shouldn't make it in the morning to serve in the
evening. The flavor seems to deteriorate if it is al-
lowed to sit that long in the refrigerator. Maybe
too much of the dressing gets absorbed.
 This leaves only the onion bread pudding,
which should be eaten hot. It is so simple to make,
especially if you have sautéed the onions in advance, that your main concern will be timing, so
you can serve dinner at a particular hour.
 And since the pudding bakes at 325 degrees,
if you have only one oven, warm the veal at the
same temperature by putting it in for the last 30
minutes of the pudding's baking time.

*Lee Bailey stainless steel flatware; Dean & Deluca
wineglass; Rosenthal white-on-white embossed porcelain plate; D. F. Sanders white textured napkin.*

Small Birthday Party

Chicken pot pie
with corn bread crust

MENU

Chicken Pot Pie with Corn Bread Crust
Watercress Salad with Egg Dressing
Cranberry Hot Pepper Sauce
Coconut Cake
Wine
Champagne
Coffee

This menu is to celebrate a special personal occasion, like a friend's birthday. The chicken pie with corn bread crust is a variation on an old dish that is marvelously satisfying and always pleases. It is accompanied by watercress salad with egg dressing and cranberry sauce laced with hot pepper jelly. To finish there is a coconut birthday cake made from a family recipe, topped with chocolate whipped cream or plain vanilla ice cream (or both?).

The fact that this is such a straightforward and homey meal is part of its appeal. But, to make things more festive, I would serve champagne with the cake.

Champagne

Coconut birthday cake

CHICKEN POT PIE WITH CORN BREAD CRUST

I have been serving chicken pot pie to mark special occasions for over fifteen years now. It never fails—there seems to be something so soothing about its flavor. And it must have pleasant memory associations for most people as well.

I've tinkered around with the combination of vegetables, the crust, and the sauce for a good many years, too. This recipe is my favorite on all scores. However, don't let that keep you from doing your own tinkering.

　1　large hen (over 3 pounds)
　10　celery stalks (with tops)
　1　cup carrot rings
　1　cup potato cubes
　1　large onion (8 ounces), thinly sliced
　6　tablespoons (¾ stick) margarine (or half butter and half margarine)
　4　cups hot chicken stock
　6　tablespoons flour
　　　Salt to taste
　½　teaspoon white pepper
　8　drops Tabasco sauce
　1　cup frozen baby lima beans

Crust
　1½　cups white cornmeal
　1½　cups flour
　2　tablespoons baking powder
　3　tablespoons sugar
　1½　teaspoons salt
　1½　cups milk
　2　eggs, slightly beaten
　¼　cup safflower oil

Put the hen in a large kettle and just cover with water. Break up the celery and put it in the pot. Simmer for 1½ hours, or until the chicken is tender. Skim if necessary. Let cool in the stock. When cool, take the chicken carefully from the stock and remove the meat, discarding the skin, but returning the bones to the pot. Measure out 4 very generous cups of chicken meat, cube, and set aside. (Refrigerate the rest of the meat, to be used later in chicken salad or the like.) Simmer the stock for another hour to reduce it. Taste it to correct the seasoning. Discard the bones. If it does not have a pronounced enough flavor, bolster it with a few chicken bouillon cubes.

Put the carrots in a saucepan and just cover with water. Simmer for 4 minutes. Drain. Set aside. Put the potatoes on, just covered with water, and simmer for 7 minutes. Drain. Set aside.

Preheat the oven to 450 degrees.

Sauté the onion in the margarine until wilted. Meanwhile, put the stock on to heat up. Stir the flour into the onion and mix well. Add the heated stock slowly, stirring or whisking constantly. When smooth, let simmer for a minute and add some salt and pepper and the Tabasco sauce.

To assemble the pie, put a layer of chicken in the bottom of a greased shallow 3-quart casserole. Sprinkle a third each of the frozen limas and cooked carrots and potatoes over it. Add salt and pepper. Repeat until all the chicken and vegetables are used. Pour the stock sauce over it all and top with the following crust:

Sift together the cornmeal, flour, baking powder, sugar, and salt. Mix the milk with the eggs and safflower oil. Mix in with the dry ingredients. Pour over the chicken and vegetables and bake for 25 minutes, or until golden brown.

Serves 8

WATERCRESS SALAD WITH EGG DRESSING

The egg dressing used with the watercress is a variation of one I've known for years, dating back to the time I lived in New Orleans. It is still one of my favorite ways of dressing salad greens.

　3　bunches watercress, washed, dried, and with tough stems broken off

Egg Dressing
　1½　tablespoons balsamic vinegar
　¾　teaspoon salt
　1　teaspoon green peppercorn mustard
　　　Dash of black pepper
　5　tablespoons safflower oil
　3　tablespoons olive oil
　2　tablespoons mayonnaise (optional)

　6　hard-boiled eggs, chopped fine or shredded

Put the watercress in a large bowl.

To make the dressing, whisk together all the remaining ingredients except the eggs. Pour enough dressing over the watercress so that when it is tossed all the greens will be generously coated. Just before serving, toss in the eggs, reserving a little to sprinkle over the top.

Serves 8

CRANBERRY HOT PEPPER SAUCE

I like the surprising kick hot pepper jelly gives cranberry sauce. You can make it as fiery as you please.

- 12 ounces fresh cranberries (1 package), washed and picked over
- 1 cup water
- 1 cup sugar
- One 4- or 5-ounce jar of jalapeño jelly

Combine the berries, water, and sugar. Cook until the berries begin to burst open. Remove from the heat and stir in the jar of jelly. Let cool and refrigerate.

Serves 8

COCONUT CAKE

This simple cake can be made in two parts. Make the cake the day before, and ice it the day of the party. Serve with Chocolate Whipped Cream (page 113).

Cake
- 1¾ cups sifted flour
- ¼ teaspoon salt
- 2½ teaspoons baking powder
- 8 tablespoons (1 stick) unsalted butter, softened
- 1 cup sugar
- 2 eggs
- ⅔ cup milk
- 1 teaspoon vanilla extract

Icing
- 1 tablespoon white corn syrup
- 1 cup sugar
- ⅓ cup water
- 1 egg white
- 1 teaspoon vanilla extract
- 1 cup plus grated fresh coconut*

Preheat the oven to 350 degrees. Lightly grease and flour two 8-inch cake pans. Set aside.

Sift the flour again with the salt and baking powder. Set aside. Using a hand mixer, cream together the butter and sugar until it is light yellow. Add the eggs, one at the time, beating after each. Add the milk and flour alternately, ending with the flour, and mixing thoroughly after each addition. Stir in the vanilla and pour into the prepared pans. Bake for 35 to 40 minutes, or until a cake tester comes out clean. Let cool in the pan, then invert onto racks.

To make the icing, put the syrup, sugar, and water in a small saucepan and bring to a brisk boil. Turn the heat down to a normal boil and cook until a candy thermometer registers between 238 and 240 degrees. This will take about 7 to 10 minutes, so you can get the egg white ready in the meantime—put it in a bowl and beat until stiff. At 238 degrees the sugar syrup will spin a very fine thread; if it goes up past 240 degrees it will harden too quickly. So at 238 degrees, pour the syrup in a steady stream into the beaten egg white, beating all the while. I use a hand mixer for this. Add the vanilla and mix it in.

Cover the top of the bottom cake layer by putting a big blob of icing in the center and coaxing it out to the edges. Sprinkle this generously with coconut. Put the top layer on very gently. You might want to secure it in place with toothpicks. Ice the top in the same way you did the bottom layer. Using a spatula (dipped in water, if necessary), ice the sides. Sprinkle the top and sides with coconut.

Serves 12

GAME PLAN

Boil the chicken and bake the cake the day before. If you have time, get the coconut grated and make the cranberry sauce. This means that on the day of the party you will only have to bake the pie and ice the cake. Assemble the pie in the afternoon and refrigerate, covered. If you do this, put the pie in a 250-degree oven, still covered, for about 30 minutes to slowly heat through before you actually bake it. The cake may also be iced several hours before the guests arrive.

Not only is this menu a reliable party pleaser, but it lets you be in the living room instead of stuck in the kitchen.

French stainless steel bistro ware; Lee Bailey wineglass; Wedgwood champagne flute; Bailey-Bannett Inc. pink oxford cloth napkin.

Vegetable Pasta Dinner

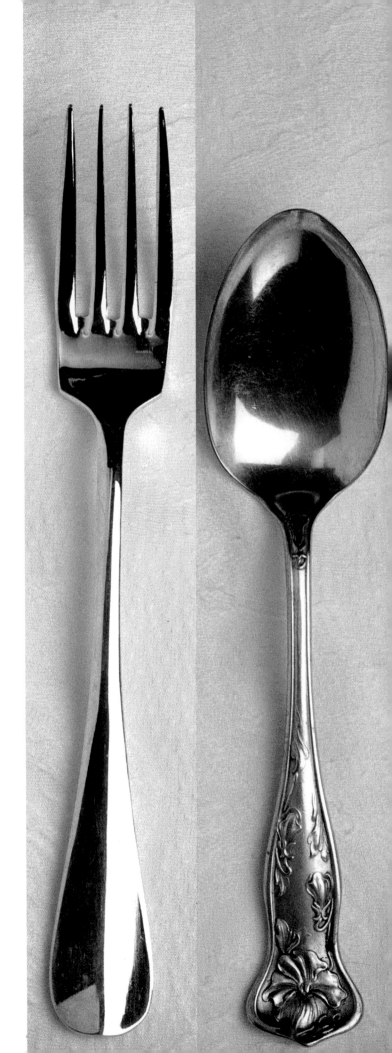

This menu is built on tomatoes, corn, peppers, and peaches—my favorites all. The tomatoes are the yellow ones, which are less acidic, and the peppers are yellow too, somewhat milder than the green. And think how beautiful the two yellows will look together when served.

For dessert there is a melting fresh peach cake.

This dinner is typical of those I make when I first return to the city, because I can prepare the sauce and bake the cake (without the filling) in the country and bring it into town.

Incidentally, one of the great joys of fall is the abundance of vegetables crowding the farm markets—a perfect time for a vegetable dinner. I've learned the secret to these special dinners, which is to balance the leafy and green vegetables with a starchy one or two. And I always serve corn bread. Of course, everything should be fresh.

Interestingly enough, the freshness of vegetables is not so important for soups. Older vegetables seem to have more flavor, making them ideal for soup.

Rigatoni with yellow tomato and corn sauce

MENU

Pasta with Yellow Tomatoes,
Peppers, and Corn
Bibb Lettuce and Cheese Salad
Crusty Bread and Sweet Butter
Fresh Peach Cake
Wine
Coffee

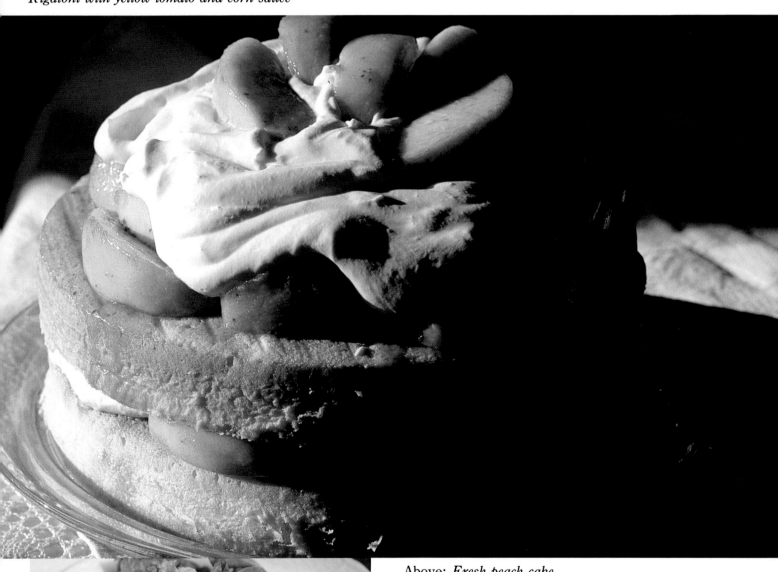

Above: *Fresh peach cake*
Left: *Lettuce and cheese salad*

PASTA WITH YELLOW TOMATOES, PEPPERS, AND CORN

Tomato sauce in almost any form freezes very well, so I make several batches to enjoy later in the year, when the snow is on the ground and the taste of good tomatoes is just a teasing memory.

If you do want to freeze this, make it up to the point of adding the corn and prosciutto. Then toss the prosciutto in the butter as directed, but do not cook the corn. Put it in the mixture raw; it will cook when the sauce is rewarmed later.

  4 medium to large onions
  2 large garlic cloves
  3 large sweet golden yellow peppers, roasted (see page 121), peeled, and seeded
  1 large light yellow pepper, roasted, peeled, and seeded
  2 tablespoons olive oil
3¼ pounds yellow tomatoes, peeled and seeded
  1 teaspoon salt
  ¼ teaspoon black pepper
 32 fresh tarragon leaves, finely chopped (about 1½ tablespoons)
  2 tablespoons finely chopped fresh parsley
  1 pound large pasta tubes (rigatoni)
  3 tablespoons unsalted butter
  4 ounces prosciutto, diced
    Kernels cut from 4 ears of corn
    Freshly grated Parmesan cheese

Roast the unpeeled onions and garlic at 425 degrees until soft to the touch. The onions will take from 1 to 1¼ hours, and the garlic cloves will take about 25 minutes. Meanwhile, give the roasted peppers a whirl in a food processor and set aside.

Peel the onions and garlic and purée them together. Heat the olive oil in a large skillet and add the onion-garlic purée. Stir to mix and add the tomatoes. Simmer them for about 25 minutes, or until they fall apart. When this is simmering briskly, add the salt, black pepper, and tarragon. Add the parsley in the last 10 minutes and stir in the puréed peppers.

Put a large pot of salted water on to boil. When it is boiling rapidly, put in the rigatoni and cook for 10 minutes. Test for tenderness. This is not good too al dente.

While the pasta is cooking, melt 2 tablespoons butter in a medium skillet and add the diced prosciutto. Sauté a minute or two to heat through and then add the corn. Cook the corn until just done. This will be only a few minutes. Add prosciutto and corn to the heated tomato mixture. Mix well.

Drain the pasta and toss with the remaining 1 tablespoon of butter. Put in individual warmed bowls and top with the sauce. Sprinkle with grated Parmesan cheese.

Serves 6

BIBB LETTUCE AND CHEESE SALAD

I don't know about your location, but for some reason, all the bibb lettuce we get around here is loaded with sand. If you have the same problem, be sure to wash it carefully. Nothing ruins a salad quicker than grit.

My method of washing is to separate the leaves in running water and then put them in a large bowl of water to soak. I then lift the lettuce out and change the water.

  ¾ teaspoon salt
  ¼ teaspoon black pepper
  1 generous teaspoon grainy mustard
  2 tablespoons fresh lemon juice
  2 tablespoons mild olive oil
  4 tablespoons safflower oil
  3 medium to large heads bibb lettuce, leaves separated, carefully washed and dried
  ¾ pound St. Albry or other soft cheese

Put the salt, pepper, and mustard in a small bowl and mix in the lemon juice. Whisk in the oils. If you do this in advance, do not refrigerate.

To serve, arrange lettuce leaves on individual plates with a slice of cheese in the middle. Spoon some of the vinaigrette over all.

Serves 6

FRESH PEACH CAKE

This recipe makes a very dense cake, which I love the flavor of. It is an old Pennsylvania Dutch recipe, I'm told, but I wouldn't swear to it. The peaches and cream are my own madness.

1½ cups heavy cream
6 tablespoons sugar
1 teaspoon vanilla extract
2 cups sifted flour
5 tablespoons plus 1 teaspoon cornstarch
2 teaspoons baking powder
¾ teaspoon salt
6 tablespoons (¾ stick) margarine
6 tablespoons (¾ stick) butter
1⅓ cups sugar
⅔ cup milk
1½ teaspoons vanilla extract
9 egg whites
4 large or 6 medium peaches
Juice of ½ small lemon
1 tablespoon sugar

Mix the cream, sugar, and vanilla and refrigerate, covered, for at least 2 hours before whipping it.

Preheat the oven to 350 degrees. Generously grease and lightly flour two 9-inch cake pans. Set aside.

Sift the flour again with the cornstarch, baking powder, and salt. Set aside.

Cream together the margarine, butter, and sugar. When light yellow, add the flour, alternating it with the milk. Begin and end with flour. Mix in the vanilla. Set aside.

Whip the egg whites until they stand in stiff peaks. Pile on top of the batter and fold in with an over-and-under motion. Do not beat, but be sure it is well mixed. Pour into the cake pans and bake in the middle of the oven for 25 to 30 minutes, or until a cake tester comes out clean. Let cool in the pans for 10 minutes before inverting onto a cake rack.

To assemble, dip the peaches in hot water for about 10 seconds, then run cold water over them. Slip off the skins and cut each into about a dozen slices. Toss the slices with lemon juice and sugar. Next, whip the cream mixture until it is stiff.

The peaches will have given up a bit of juice by now, so pour some of it over the bottom layer, a little at a time to let it soak in. Put half the slices on this bottom layer and cover with whipped cream. Place the second layer on top and repeat, saving a few peach slices for garnish. You may have to hold this second layer in place with a couple of toothpicks.

Serves 8 to 12

GAME PLAN

As I said above, I almost always make a double batch of this tomato sauce and freeze half for later. You might want to do the same.

If you have time, make the sauce up to the point of adding the prosciutto and corn in the mid-afternoon and complete it just before you are ready to serve.

Salad greens should be washed, dried, and stored in the refrigerator, wrapped in paper towels. Mix the salad dressing and set aside.

Bake the cake, but do not assemble it until just before your guests are due; the lemon juice on the peaches will keep them from getting discolored. Once assembled, however, you should refrigerate the cake, because of the whipped cream. Drape a piece of waxed paper over the top. Don't try to wrap it.

It is very simple to double all these recipes for larger groups, and the cake already may be stretched to serve 12. However, if you need more dessert, make two cakes.

Wolfman-Gold unmatched antique silverplate flatware; Baccarat cut crystal goblet; Tiffany white-on-white porcelain plate and saucer; Wolfman-Gold white napkin with lace trim.

Turkey breast slices, marinated tomatoes, and rice

*Chocolate angel food cake
with Irish coffee sauce
and whipped cream*

Summer Dinner in Winter

MENU

*Turkey Breast with Marinated Tomatoes
Baked Wild Rice and Dried Mushrooms
Chocolate Angel Food Cake with
Irish Coffee Sauce
Wine
Coffee*

Nothing reminds me more of deep summer than tomatoes—and during the bleakest weeks of winter, usually right after the first of the year, a craving for their memory-nudging flavor overtakes me. But sadly, as we all do, I have discovered that although the markets at this time of year display a tempting variety of authentic-looking specimens, their taste disappoints more often than not. Luckily, sometime along the way I also discovered that small cherry tomatoes come closer than any other to tasting vine-ripened. And by adding a good olive oil and fresh basil, which I sometimes grow in my kitchen window, I can come up with a tasty salad that satisfies the taste buds. This salad, with the addition of Italian red onions and a generous grind of black pepper, makes the topping for an interesting way of serving sautéed turkey slices.

TURKEY BREAST WITH MARINATED TOMATOES

The sliced turkey breast in this recipe is used very much like scallops of veal. As a matter of fact, most people think it is veal unless you tell them otherwise. The marinated raw tomatoes that top it off are a visual treat and make the dish almost a meal in itself.

By the way, make sure your butcher gives you the turkey bones with any bits of meat left over when he slices the breast. This makes a very tasty soup. See page 96.

Marinated Tomatoes

- 6 cups cherry tomatoes, washed and cut in half
- 1 cup coarsely chopped red onion
- 8 to 10 large basil leaves, cut into thin strips
- ½ cup extra-virgin olive oil
  Several grinds of black pepper
  Salt

- 2 cups soft bread crumbs
  Flour
- 2 eggs (or 1 cup Egg Beaters)
- 3 tablespoons olive oil
- 3 tablespoons butter or 1 tablespoon butter and 2 tablespoons margarine
- 1¾ to 2 pounds turkey breast, sliced as for scallopini
  Salt and pepper to taste

Mix together the tomatoes, onion, basil, olive oil, and pepper. Set aside. (Ideally, this should be done a few hours in advance to give the flavor a chance to mature. If you refrigerate it, let it come back to room temperature before serving. Add the salt at the very end.)

Tear off two sheets of waxed paper and place them on a surface next to the stove. Put the bread crumbs on the side closer to the skillet and the flour on the other side. Lightly beat the eggs and put them in a flat plate large enough to hold a slice of turkey. Put this between the two sheets of paper, so that the coating ingredients are lined up: flour, eggs, bread crumbs. Put half the oil and butter in a large skillet. When ready to start cooking, dredge a slice of breast in flour, shaking off the excess. Next dip it in egg and let it drain a bit when you lift it. Finally, coat it with bread crumbs. When half the slices are coated, turn on the heat under the oil and butter. When this is very foamy, put the slices in and give them a sprinkling of salt and pepper. While they are cooking, coat the other slices and set aside. Turn the slices as they start to brown. This should only take 3 or 4 minutes in all. Remove the pan from the heat after you have cooked the first batch and add the rest of the oil and butter. If the butter from the previous batch has burned, wipe the pan out before adding fresh butter and oil. Return the pan to the heat and repeat the process. If you must do this in three batches, you may have to add more oil and butter. Keep the slices warm, but serve them as soon as possible.

Top each serving with a generous portion of marinated tomatoes.

Serves 6

BAKED WILD RICE AND DRIED MUSHROOMS

Because wild rice is so expensive, I stretch it a bit by mixing it with regular rice. You still get the distinctive taste and texture of wild rice, but at half the cost.

- ¾ cup wild rice, washed carefully
- ¾ cup long-grain white rice
  Chicken stock
- 1 ounce dried Italian mushrooms
- ¼ cup sherry

Preheat the oven to 350 degrees. Generously butter a deep-sided casserole or soufflé dish.

Bring 3 cups salted water to a boil. Stir in the wild rice. Turn the heat down to a simmer and cook, uncovered, for 40 minutes. (Or if you have a favorite method of cooking this kind of rice, use it.) Meanwhile, in another pot cover the white rice with chicken stock to about an inch above the rice. Bring to a boil and turn the heat down to a simmer, stirring occasionally. Cook for 10 minutes. Drain in a colander and rinse with hot water. Set aside.

Cover the dried mushrooms with hot water. After about 20 minutes drain them, reserving the liquid for another use, and chop coarsely. Sauté for 3 or 4 minutes in a little butter and then pour in the sherry. Simmer until the liquid evaporates. Combine the mushrooms with the white rice. Drain off any excess liquid from the wild rice. Mix it with the other ingredients and pour into the casserole. Bake set in a pan of hot water for 20 minutes. Let it sit for a few minutes after removing it from the oven. Loosen the edges with a knife and invert onto a serving plate. Sometimes this can be temperamental. In that case, pack it back into the casserole to serve.

Note: Mushroom liquid, after being strained through a doubled piece of cheesecloth or a coffee filter, may be used in soup or sauces.

Serves 6 to 8

CHOCOLATE ANGEL FOOD CAKE

Almost all recipes for basic angel food cake are the same, the only variations being slight: the quantities of sugar, egg white, and flour. The most important things about making this particular cake are being sure that the cocoa is well mixed in with the flour and letting the cake cool after baking. Otherwise, it is simplicity itself and will keep very well. Although it is sometimes difficult to find plain cake flour, do not use the self-rising kind in its place.

  ¾ cup sifted cake flour
  4 generous tablespoons cocoa
1¼ cups egg whites, at room temperature
  ¼ teaspoon salt
  1 teaspoon cream of tartar
1¼ cups sifted sugar
  1 teaspoon vanilla extract or lemon juice
     Irish Coffee Sauce (recipe follows)
  ½ pint heavy cream, whipped

Garnish
  Powdered espresso

Put a rack in the center of the oven and preheat the oven to 375 degrees.

Tear off two squares of waxed paper. Put the flour and cocoa in a sifter and sift onto one of the squares. Repeat this process, going back and forth between squares, until the flour and cocoa are well mixed—four or five times. Set aside.

Beat the egg whites and salt together for a few seconds and then sprinkle on the cream of tartar. Continue beating until stiff. Fold in the sugar, a little at a time, with an over-and-under motion, always in the same direction. Fold in the vanilla. Fold in the flour-cocoa mixture, also a little at a time, but don't take too long to finish. Pour the batter into an ungreased 10-inch tube pan and bake for 30 minutes, until a cake tester inserted in the center comes out clean. Let cool completely before removing from pan.

To serve, put a slick of Irish coffee sauce on each dessert plate and on top of that a slice of cake (cut the cake with a bread knife). Finish it off by spooning whipped cream over the top and dusting on some of the powdered espresso.

Serves 12

IRISH COFFEE SAUCE

1 cup sugar
7 tablespoons water
1 cup freshly made coffee
2 tablespoons Irish whiskey or bourbon

Put the sugar and water in a fairly large saucepan and bring to a boil. Simmer, stirring, for about 10 minutes, until the mixture begins to turn a caramel color. Toward the end of the cooking time it will become very foamy as it starts to darken. Be sure to stir constantly at this point, and just as it becomes a medium caramel color, turn off heat but continue to stir—it will become darker even off the heat. Then add the coffee. Be careful here, as the mixture tends to spatter when the coffee first makes contact. (That is why you need to do this in a large pan.) Mix well and let cool. Stir in the whiskey and refrigerate in a glass container.

Makes 2½ cups

GAME PLAN

Start preparing this meal by making the cake in the afternoon. Then do the wild rice casserole and set it aside without baking. Next, mix the tomatoes with their other ingredients and let them marinate. Try to time yourself so that these last two finish about when your guests are due to arrive. If you can, you might also set up the coating ingredients for the turkey slices, but sautéing them is best done just before serving. The wild rice should be put in the oven to come out a little before you plan to finish the turkey.

Conran's white-handled stainless steel flatware; Kosta-Boda wineglass; Coalport porcelain dinner plate; Wolfman-Gold white waffleweave piqué napkin.

Lunch for a Cold Sunday Afternoon

Above: *Turkey vegetable soup*
Right: *Swiss cheese and arugula salad*

To my way of thinking, planning a lunch around warming soup can create one of the most satisfying of meals. And when I am lucky enough to have turkey bones in the freezer (see page 92) to start the soup with, I know my guests will be in for a treat. So this is the kind of lunch I like to serve in the middle of a Sunday afternoon when the weather outside is blustery and the mood inside is warm. For such occasions always be sure to have plenty of whatever soup you make, along with several kinds of good bread and sweet butter to start. Then follow with salad, in this case a delicious creation by André Soltner of Lutèce. To finish, my choice is a hearty cobbler, with which I serve the coffee, instead of serving it after the dessert, as I usually do.

Cold Sundays have also always seemed a good time to stir up special mixed drinks. You might try the applejack and champagne concoction I've given a recipe for here; it's delicious. Another interesting cold-weather mixer is apple cider. I've had it with aquavit—but for some people aquavit is definitely an acquired taste, so maybe it is safer to just pour a generous jigger of vodka over crushed ice and add the apple cider, a dash of bitters, and a twist of lemon and let it go at that. The only caution here is not to serve *too* many, because mixed drinks can be more lethal than ordinary highballs or wine.

MENU

Turkey Vegetable Soup
Swiss Cheese Salad
Assorted Breads with Sweet Butter
Apricot Cobbler
Champagne and Applejack
Coffee

Apricot cobbler for dessert

TURKEY VEGETABLE SOUP

This soup has a few surprising elements in it. Just be sure to brown the turkey meat and bones properly and make certain that the chicken stock is nice and flavorful. I like to season my chicken stock before I put it in with the other ingredients so that I won't have to try to figure out how to correct the seasoning later.

    2 tablespoons safflower oil
    1 raw turkey breast carcass with meat on bones,
      chopped roughly into 4 or 5 pieces
      Four 13½ ounce cans chicken broth (or
      approximately 7 cups homemade stock),
      seasoning corrected if necessary
    4 cups water
    ½ very large red onion, peeled and thinly sliced
    2 cups snapped green beans, puréed to the
      consistency of relish
    1½ pounds white potatoes, peeled and cubed
    4 large parsley sprigs (without stems), chopped
    ½ teaspoon black pepper
      One 10-ounce box frozen peas

In the safflower oil, carefully and thoroughly brown (but do not burn) the turkey carcass parts and any bits of leftover raw meat. This may take about 5 minutes or more. Add the broth and water. Bring to a simmer and continue to cook for about 40 minutes, skimming occasionally. Remove the bones and meat and let them cool. Remove the meat from the bones and chop it coarsely. Discard the bones.

  Add the onion and green beans to the liquid and simmer over very low heat. Add the potatoes and set a timer for 5 minutes. Add the parsley and pepper. (The black pepper is very important here, so don't be shy about the amount.) Add the reserved turkey meat and simmer just long enough to finish cooking the potatoes. Add the peas and continue cooking for just a minute or two to heat them through.

Serves 8 generously

Note: This soup can be frozen with no loss in flavor, although the potatoes and peas get a little mushy. Should you want to prepare this soup well in advance, do it up to the time you put in the potatoes and peas and complete this last step just before serving.

SWISS CHEESE SALAD

You should not substitute any other green in this delightful salad, as the bite of arugula is very important. A milder-flavored lettuce cannot stand up to the potent taste of the cheese mixture.

    1½ pounds imported Swiss cheese, shredded
       on a grater
    3 tablespoons grainy mustard (preferably
       Moutarde de Meaux)
    1½ tablespoons red wine vinegar
    ¾ teaspoon black pepper
    ¼ teaspoon salt
    ½ cup olive oil
    1 bunch arugula, washed and dried

Put the cheese in a bowl. In another bowl make the vinaigrette by combining the mustard, vinegar, pepper, and salt, and then whisking in the oil. When ready to serve, add the dressing to the cheese and toss very lightly and carefully with two forks. Arrange several sprigs of arugula on each plate and mound the cheese in the middle.

Serves 8

APRICOT COBBLER

As anyone who knows me can tell you, fruit cobblers are among my favorite desserts. I often make a cobbler of apricots when they turn up in the market. I love their tartness, but because this can sometimes be overwhelming, I usually add a large apple or a couple of peaches. Also, apricots are a pain in the neck to peel, so having fewer to do is welcome. Even when the apricots are dipped in hot water, their skins don't just slide off as easily as peach skins do. And if they are slightly green, they are hard to pit. Anyway, don't let my complaining dissuade you. The cobbler is worth the little extra work.

    1½ cups flour
       Scant ¼ teaspoon salt
    5 tablespoons unsalted butter, frozen
    4 tablespoons Crisco, frozen
    4 to 5 tablespoons ice water

    2½ pounds ripe apricots
    1 large Granny Smith apple or 2 large peaches
    1 cup sugar
    4 tablespoons (½ stick) unsalted butter
    ½ pint heavy cream, whipped

Preheat the oven to 450 degrees. Lightly grease a 1½- to 2-quart ovenproof dish.

To make the cobbler pastry, put flour and salt in a food processor. Add the frozen butter and Crisco and process to the size of small peas. Add 4 tablespoons ice water and process until the dough begins to cling together (this shouldn't take too long—10 seconds or so). If more water is required, add it. Gather the dough into a ball. Put it between two sheets of waxed paper and flatten the ball. Refrigerate it while you prepare the fruit.

Dip the apricots (and peaches) in boiling water. Let them stay in for about 10 seconds, a bit longer if they are not too ripe. Remove from the water and peel. Remove the pits and cut the flesh into thick slices. If an apple is being used, peel and core it and thickly slice.

Roll out the dough on a floured surface, making a large ragged circle. Since handling it can be a bit ungainly, dust it with flour and roll it up on your rolling pin (window-shade fashion). Unroll it over the prepared dish. Carefully slip it down in place so that you have lined the bottom and sides, allowing the excess to hang over the edge.

Heap the apricot and peach or apple slices into the dish, mounding them in the middle. Cover with the sugar and dot with the 4 tablespoons butter. Flop the loose ends of the pastry over the top. Any extra loose pieces of dough can be used to fill in. Put it in the preheated oven and turn the heat down to 425 degrees. Bake for 45 minutes. Let cool and serve with whipped cream (or plain cream or ice cream).

Serves 8

CHAMPAGNE AND APPLEJACK

For those of you who don't know, applejack is apple brandy, an American cousin to French calvados. Combined with champagne, it makes an awfully good (and potent) drink.

Simple syrup
    Sugar
    Water

    Applejack
    Champagne
    Lemon twists (optional)

To make simple syrup, which is used in many mixed drinks, combine equal amounts of sugar and water. Bring to a boil. Turn off the heat, and when the mixture is cool, refrigerate it in a tightly sealed jar. It keeps almost indefinitely.

Have all other ingredients chilled, as well as the glasses. Put ½ teaspoon of simple syrup in each champagne flute (or more, according to taste) along with half a jigger of applejack. Fill the glass with champagne. Stir once to mix, no more, as too much stirring will dissipate the bubbles in the wine. If you like, run a lemon twist around the rim of each glass and then twist it over the drink. Let the twist float on the top.

GAME PLAN

This lunch is dear to my heart because it can almost all be prepared in advance, timed to finish an hour or so before the guests arrive, with very little assembling at the last minute. But I don't especially suggest doing it the day before, except maybe the first few steps of the soup preparation.

Plan to bake the cobbler last, so that it will still be a bit warm when you serve it. And the soup should be made only up to the point where you are ready to add the potatoes and peas. It can wait indefinitely there, unrefrigerated (on a cool windowsill?). Potatoes may be peeled and cubed, covered with water, and set aside. Ingredients for the salad should be ready to be combined. Leave the vinaigrette out at room temperature. Ditto the cheese. If you can remember, take the butter out when you start to finish these various things so it can soften up a bit and be easy to spread. The cream can be whipped at any odd moment and refrigerated; give it a stir before serving if it has been in the refrigerator for a while, as it tends to separate.

French stainless steel bistro ware; Val St. Lambert wineglass; Metropolitan Museum of Art porcelain plate; Frank McIntosh ecru linen napkin.

Yogurt-mustard chicken with potatoes, carrots, and turnips

Winter Chicken Dinner

Tangerine mousse with blackberry sauce

Yogurt-mustard chicken is the sort of dish, because of the lack of attention its preparation requires, that is perfect to serve during the week when you are faced with a busy schedule (but still want to entertain). To go with the chicken you might do a rice pilaf cooked on top of the stove and a steamed vegetable. Dessert could be a plain mixture of winter fruit, or you could even serve something store-bought.

This menu is built around the simple yogurt-mustard chicken, but I have accompanied it with what I think are more interesting ways of preparing the vegetables—and a scrumptious dessert that is almost as easy as the chicken (and may be made the night before).

YOGURT–GREEN PEPPERCORN MUSTARD CHICKEN

This dish is not only extremely easy to prepare, but has the advantage of being able to sit in the oven for an almost indefinite time after the heat is turned off. I've actually let it go for almost two hours and it was still fine, coming out moist and warm. Not piping hot, of course, but I like the flavor of chicken better when it isn't very hot anyway.

  8 chicken thighs
  2 whole chicken breasts, split in half
     Salt and black pepper to taste
  6 generous tablespoons plain yogurt
  2 scant tablespoons green peppercorn mustard

Preheat the oven to 375 degrees.

With foil, line a pan just large enough to hold the 8 thighs snugly. You may crowd them together. Line another pan for the breasts in the same way. Salt and pepper the chicken on all sides.

Combine the yogurt and mustard and paint the undersides of the chicken parts generously with the mixture. Put the chicken, skin side up, in the pans, making sure the skin is stretched over them completely. Paint the tops with the remaining sauce.

Bake in the oven for 35 minutes. Then turn off the oven, but do not open the door. Let them continue to cook by retained heat for another hour. Chicken may remain in the oven even longer if necessary.

Serves 6

CANDIED CARROTS AND TURNIPS

Carrots and turnips are a nice duo. Their flavors complement each other well, especially when they are lightly glazed. But if the prospect of glazing doesn't strike your fancy, you can always just squeeze a lemon over them and add a dab of butter instead.

  1 pound carrots, scraped and cut into rings
  1 pound turnips, peeled and cut into rings
  4 tablespoons (½ stick) unsalted butter
  4 tablespoons granulated brown sugar

Steam the carrots and turnips separately for about 6 minutes each, until tender. Salt very lightly.

Melt the butter in a large skillet and add the brown sugar. Mix well and add the vegetables. Continue to cook gently for 4 minutes, turning until well glazed.

Note: You may steam the carrots and turnips a little in advance and use the glazing to heat them through.

Serves 6

SCOTTISH SKILLET POTATOES

I don't know why these are called Scottish potatoes, but the person who told me how to make them called them that, and the name stuck in my head. They require only slight attention, except that you mustn't let them burn as the liquid reduces. So keep an eye on the flame.

  1 thick bacon slice, cut into small pieces
  1 medium onion, thinly sliced
  2 tablespoons (¼ stick) unsalted butter
  2 pounds potatoes, peeled and cut into
     ½-inch slices
  1 teaspoon salt in 1 cup hot water
  ¼ teaspoon black pepper

In a very large skillet with a lid (so you can spread the potatoes out in one layer), sauté the bacon until it is almost done. Add the onion, and when it has wilted, add the butter, potatoes, and salted water. Sprinkle on the pepper and cover. Bring to a boil and cook over a very low flame for 20 minutes. Uncover and continue cooking for another 12 to 15 minutes, shaking the pan occasionally. At the end most of the liquid should be gone and the bottoms of the potatoes turning golden. Let them rest for an additional 10 minutes, covered, before serving.

Serves 6

TANGERINE MOUSSE

I am very partial to the flavor of tangerines; it is not as sharp as that of regular oranges. And now that tangerine juice can be bought frozen, this dessert almost makes itself.

Practically any kind of berry could be used for the sauce, either fresh or frozen. This is one instance when frozen berries work fine, and they are likely to be cheaper than fresh. I used blackberries because I had them, but blueberries or raspberries would do as well.

  6 eggs, separated
  ½ cup sugar
  1 tablespoon gelatin
  1 cup frozen tangerine juice concentrate, thawed
    Grated rind of 1 orange
  2 tablespoons Grand Marnier
  1 cup heavy cream
  4 tablespoons confectioners' sugar
  ¼ teaspoon cream of tartar
  ¼ teaspoon salt
    Berry Sauce (recipe follows)

Garnish
    Fresh berries

Put the egg yolks in a bowl with the sugar and gelatin. Beat until light in color and thickened. Pour this into the top of a double boiler and add the juice and orange rind. Heat just enough to dissolve the gelatin and sugar. Do not allow to boil, or the egg might curdle. Set aside to cool. When cool, stir in the Grand Marnier.

Start whipping the cream and then add the confectioners' sugar. Continue whipping until the cream forms stiff peaks. Pour it over the egg-juice mixture. Fold in carefully.

Whip the egg whites until foamy, then add the cream of tartar and salt. Continue whipping until it forms *soft* peaks. Fold this into the other mixture. Pour into a 6-cup soufflé dish and refrigerate, covered with plastic wrap, until set—or better still, overnight. Serve with berry sauce and garnish with a few fresh berries.

Note: For a more impressive presentation, use a soufflé dish with shorter sides and tie a lightly oiled parchment paper collar around it (or use plain waxed paper). When you remove the collar, the soufflé will have set and be sticking up slightly above the dish.

Serves 6 to 8

BERRY SAUCE

This is made by simmering a box of fresh or frozen berries (blackberries, blueberries, raspberries, or strawberries) with ¼ to ½ cup of sugar (depending on how sweet you like it) for about 5 minutes, or until it starts to thicken very slightly. You want to be able to pour the sauce easily when it is cool. Strain out the seeds with a fine sieve (not necessary with blueberries) and refrigerate.

GAME PLAN

The mousse and sauce should be the first things you make for this meal, preferably the night before, but at least 4 hours in advance.

Next is the chicken, which must go into a preheated oven but then can be almost ignored. When you decide what time you would like to serve dinner, give yourself a half hour and go in and prepare the potatoes. I would peel them in advance, so I would have just the actual cooking to deal with. After these are done, set them aside for their 10-minute resting period and get to the carrots and turnips. They should all be ready at about the same time.

David Mellor black plastic-handled and stainless steel flatware; Simon Pearce hand-blown Irish glass goblet; Gwathmey Siegel for Swid Powell black-and-white porcelain plate; D. F. Sanders ocher linen napkin.

Crawfish Pasta Dinner

Above: *Several of the ingredients for this meal.* Below: *Pasta with crawfish sauce*

MENU

Whole Baby Eggplant in Oil
Pasta with Crawfish Sauce
Boston Lettuce Salad with Sherry
Vinaigrette
Blackberry Roll
Wine
Coffee

A few times a year I treat myself to crawfish (crayfish is called crawfish in the South, where they come from) brought in from my native Louisiana. In some locations they can be bought live, but when these are not available, often fish markets can get frozen crawfish tails if you ask for them in advance. One of my favorite ways of eating them is in a sauce for pasta. And since this makes a very rich dish, it is best served when the weather is cool in the fall or early spring.

So few people outside of the South know what crawfish tastes like that it is fun to serve it to guests on a special occasion. And to make the meal even more special I might just use some of my precious frozen blackberries to make a blackberry roll for dessert.

The meal starts with broiled baby eggplant, mainly because I like it prepared that way. But this menu is so hearty that if you don't want to bother with this first course, your guests will certainly be none the wiser.

Grilled eggplant in oil

WHOLE BABY EGGPLANT IN OIL

If you have a sunny patch on your back steps or on a terrace, you can easily grow these delicious little eggplants. They thrive in pots, and one or two bushes will provide you with more eggplants in season than you can use. At any rate, they are usually available year round in the markets.

12 small, "finger" eggplants (each approximately 4½ inches long)
¼ cup olive oil
3 large garlic cloves, cut in half
¼ cup chicken stock
2 teaspoons soy sauce
Lemon juice
Salt and black pepper to taste

Cut each eggplant in half, leaving it attached at the stem on top. Sprinkle the flesh with salt and set aside in the refrigerator for 30 minutes.

Heat the oil in a large skillet and add the garlic. Fry the garlic until it is almost golden. Wipe the eggplants dry and add them, flesh side down, to the pan with the garlic. Cook the eggplants over medium heat for several minutes. Add the stock and soy sauce. Cover and simmer for 6 or 7 minutes. Test for doneness on the flesh side.

Place eggplants on a platter and make an incision down the length of each half. Squeeze lemon juice over all and pour the pan oil on top of this. Add salt and pepper.

Serve either hot or at room temperature.

Serves 6

PASTA WITH CRAWFISH SAUCE

Crawfish is generally prepared with a brown tomatoey sauce in almost all its incarnations. This recipe is typical of the way they are cooked throughout Louisiana, only there, more cayenne pepper is used. So add as much as you like, but if you are not familiar with it use a light touch, because a little cayenne can be mighty powerful.

Don't be put off by the long list of ingredients in this recipe. It is a lot easier to prepare than you might think. When choosing pasta for this dish, use something with a shape that will capture some of the sauce in it, like spirals or shells. There are many to choose from.

2 tablespoons (¼ stick) unsalted butter
2 tablespoons safflower oil
4 tablespoons flour

½ cup finely chopped shallots
1 cup finely chopped onion
¾ cup finely chopped green pepper
¾ cup finely chopped celery
2 tablespoons finely chopped celery leaves (optional)
3 cups fish stock
2 large garlic cloves, crushed
2 cups cooked crawfish tails,* with fat if possible
1 tablespoon tomato paste
1 tablespoon Worcestershire sauce
2 teaspoons fresh lemon juice
1 teaspoon salt
1 teaspoon black pepper
⅛ teaspoon cayenne pepper
1 tablespoon capers
1 tablespoon chopped fresh parsley
1 pound shaped pasta
Chopped green onion tops

Put the butter and oil in a skillet with the flour and cook slowly, moving it around with the back of a pancake turner, until it turns golden brown. Immediately add the vegetables and continue to cook, stirring and scraping the bottom, for 5 minutes or so, until they are wilted. In the meantime, put on the fish stock to heat. When the vegetables have wilted, add about 2 cups of stock and stir as it thickens. Add the garlic and crawfish. Stir and then add the tomato paste, Worcestershire sauce, lemon juice, salt, black and cayenne pepper. Add the rest of the stock and simmer for about 5 minutes more. Add the capers and parsley. Set aside.

Cook the pasta in a large quantity of salted water until al dente. Drain it, then dump it back in the hot pot and mix with a little butter. Divide it among individual warmed bowls and top with the crawfish sauce. Sprinkle with chopped green onion tops. Do not add cheese.

Serves 6

*If you are using frozen crawfish tails, cook them just as you would shrimp.

BOSTON LETTUCE SALAD WITH SHERRY VINAIGRETTE

I rather like the sweetish taste of this vinaigrette after the richness of the pasta, but if you don't have sherry vinegar, don't buy it just for this vinaigrette—unless you are unfamiliar with its flavor and want to taste it. A good red wine vinegar is a perfectly acceptable substitute.

Sherry Vinaigrette

½ teaspoon salt
¼ teaspoon black pepper
1 teaspoon Dijon mustard
2 tablespoons sherry vinegar
3 tablespoons safflower oil
2 tablespoons olive oil
3 small or 2 large heads Boston lettuce, washed, with leaves separated

Put the salt, pepper, and mustard in a small bowl and add the vinegar. Mix. Whisk in the oils. (If you are not using this right away, do not refrigerate.)

To serve, arrange the lettuce on individual salad plates and spoon a little of the vinaigrette over each.

Serves 6

BLACKBERRY ROLL

Every year I go on a blackberry hunt. They are one of my favorite berries for pies and ices. And when blackberries are plentiful, I freeze them in measured batches just large enough to make specific dishes.

2¼ cups flour
¾ cup plus 2 tablespoons sugar
1½ teaspoons salt
½ pound (2 sticks) unsalted butter, cut into small bits
4½ tablespoons ice water
4 cups blackberries
2 tablespoons melted butter
½ cup hot water

Preheat the oven to 350 degrees.

Put the flour, 2 tablespoons sugar, salt, and three fourths of the butter in a food processor. Process to a coarse texture. Add the ice water and continue to process until mixture is just beginning to form a ball. Remove it, make it into a ball, and place between two sheets of waxed paper, pressing the ball flat before refrigerating it.

Combine 3 cups of the berries and the remaining ¾ cup sugar and set aside.

Roll out the dough on a floured surface to the thickness of a piecrust. Cut out a rectangle about 9 by 15 inches. Discard any leftover dough. Brush the dough with the melted butter and spoon on the berries. Dot with the remaining bits of butter and roll up as you would a jelly roll. Place this, seam side down, in a greased baking dish. Cut several diagonal slits in the top of the roll. Sprinkle the top with additional sugar and then arrange the remaining cup of berries around the roll. Bake at 450 degrees for 10 minutes and then pour the hot water around the roll. Turn the heat down to 350 degrees and bake for another 40 to 45 minutes.

Serve slices with juice spooned on top.

Serves 6

GAME PLAN

The first thing to do is make the pasta sauce up to the point where the crawfish tails are added. It may be set aside here, or refrigerated if you are making it several hours in advance.

After the sauce is out of the way, make the blackberry roll. The sooner you eat it after it comes out of the oven, the better it is. Or you may leave it to sit in a warm oven (not hot—you don't want to cook it, just keep it warm) while you are having dinner.

Wash the salad greens and make the salad dressing. Leave the dressing unrefrigerated.

About the time guests are due to arrive, put on the water for the pasta and let it sit over the lowest possible flame. That way, when you want to start all you have to do is turn the flame up and you have boiling water in a few minutes.

If you are doing the eggplant, it can be cooked about now, as it may be served at room temperature.

You might let everyone eat this first course in the living room while you heat the sauce and cook the pasta. About the time you are ready, they will be too. If you want to have the first course with your guests, do so and then get back into the kitchen to finish the rest of the dinner, which will take 10 to 15 minutes.

It is better for guests to have that wait between courses in the living room than at the table.

Patino-Wolf polished and unpolished stainless steel flatware; Wolfman-Gold glass tumbler; Waldo Collection cement gray plate; D. F. Sanders natural and khaki checked napkin.

Easy Fish Dinner

W hat makes this dinner so easy is that the fish just needs to be rubbed with soy sauce and baked. It is accompanied by rice and pasta, simmered together just before the fish starts cooking. And the carrot-cauliflower purée can be done in advance and be waiting in a double boiler to be reheated.

Salad is nothing more than slicing cucumbers. And dessert is blackberry ice and cookies, both made in advance.

This menu can take almost any substitutions you could care to make. Although the dishes work well together as it stands, you could easily make a different purée and boil a few potatoes to go with the fish, instead of the rice and pasta. And changing desserts is never a problem so far as I am concerned.

MENU

Baked Monkfish
Rice and Pasta
Carrots and Cauliflower Purée (page 116)
Cucumber and Mint Salad
Blackberry Ice
Peanut Butter Cookies
Wine
Coffee

Aunt Freddie's peanut butter cookies

BAKED MONKFISH

Monkfish has a texture more like lobster than any other fish I know of. It doesn't flake, as most do, and it slices very nicely once it is baked.

M. F. K. Fisher is responsible for this recipe, because I read once that she said she almost always rubbed fish with soy sauce before baking it. It seemed like a good idea, so I tried it. Now I do the same.

> 3 pounds monkfish (pieces all the same
>   thickness, if possible)
>   Soy sauce
> 2 tablespoons (¼ stick) unsalted butter
>   Fresh lemon juice
>   Lemon slices

Preheat the oven to 450 degrees.

Rub the fish very generously all over with soy sauce and let it come to room temperature. With foil, line a pan large enough to hold all the fish in one layer. Grease the foil lightly. Place the fish in the pan and bake for 7 minutes for each half inch of thickness.

Meanwhile, melt the butter. When the fish is done, squeeze lemon juice liberally over all and then pour on the butter. Baste with some of the pan juices.

Serve with lemon slices.

Serves 6

RICE AND PASTA

Cooking rice and pasta together is just a way of getting a little variety. Either one separately would be fine.

> 3 tablespoons unsalted butter
> ¼ cup finely chopped onion
> 1½ cups rice
> 1½ cups spaghettini, broken into ½-inch pieces
> 4 cups fish stock or chicken stock, heated

Melt the butter in a large skillet. Add the onion and sauté for several minutes, until slightly wilted. Add the rice and spaghettini. Sauté, stirring, over moderate heat until the rice is turning white and the pasta begins to darken. Do not let burn.

Add about 2 cups of the hot stock. Stir and simmer until this is absorbed. Add more as needed. Do not boil. Test for doneness after about 15 minutes. If not, simmer for another 5 minutes.

Serves 6

CUCUMBER AND MINT SALAD

Cucumbers seem to me to be a natural accompaniment to almost any variety of fish, and yogurt marries to the cucumber as well as cucumber does to fish.

Sometimes if I peel and seed the cucumber in advance, I will salt them and put them in the refrigerator to draw out a good bit of their water. Of course, this changes their texture, making them less crunchy, but I like them that way.

> 3 cucumbers (approximately 18 ounces) peeled,
>   seeded, and cut into half-moons
> 1 tablespoon very finely chopped mint leaves
> ½ cup plain yogurt
> 4 tablespoons rice wine vinegar
> 1 teaspoon brown sugar
> ⅛ teaspoon white pepper
>   Salt to taste

Put the cucumbers in a bowl and mix with the mint. In another bowl combine all the remaining ingredients. Put the cucumbers on small individual plates and spoon some of the yogurt dressing over them.

Serves 6

BLACKBERRY ICE

During their season, I try to get enough blackberries so that I can make syrup to keep in the freezer. Should you do this, it is best to freeze the juice in quantities just large enough to make a batch of berry ice, so you won't have to defrost the whole thing each time you want to make it.

> 2 cups blackberries
> ¾ cup sugar
> 1 teaspoon lemon juice
> ¾ cup water

Put the blackberries and sugar in a small enameled pan and bring to a boil. Simmer for about 5 minutes and then add the lemon juice. Using a very fine sieve, strain out the seeds. You may put this aside at this point or freeze it for later use.

To make the ice, add the water to the syrup and pour into several metal ice-cube trays (without the dividers). Stir every 20 or 30 minutes as it begins to freeze. If it gets too solid, break it up and put in a food processor for a few whirls.

You may, of course, make the ice in an electric ice-cream maker.

PEANUT BUTTER COOKIES

This is my Aunt Freddie's recipe, and one that I use all the time. These are the simplest cookies imaginable, and have a taste that most of us associate with our childhoods. They also freeze quite well. When I freeze them, I don't even thaw them out before serving them.

½ pound (2 sticks) unsalted butter, softened
1 cup sugar
1 cup brown sugar
1 cup chunky peanut butter
2 eggs, well beaten
2½ cups flour
¾ teaspoon baking soda
Pinch of salt
1 teaspoon vanilla extract

Put the butter, sugars, and peanut butter in a bowl. Cream thoroughly. Add the eggs and mix well. Sift the flour, baking soda, and salt into the mixture. Blend well. Add the vanilla and mix. Roll into a long loaf. Roll up in waxed paper or plastic wrap and refrigerate for 24 hours. (You can make two rolls and freeze one.)

To bake, preheat the oven to 350 degrees.

Cut cookies from roll and bake on a lightly greased cookie sheet for 12 to 15 minutes.

Makes approximately 50 cookies

MISSISSIPPI MOLASSES COOKIES*

This recipe was given to me by Mrs. Curtis McCaskill of Laurel, Mississippi, a local lady whose cooking skills are well known in the area. The cookies keep very well in an airtight container.

2 cups flour
2 teaspoons baking soda
½ teaspoon salt
1 tablespoon allspice
1 teaspoon cinnamon
1 teaspoon black pepper
12 tablespoons (1½ sticks) unsalted butter
1 cup sugar
1 egg
¼ cup molasses
Extra-fine granulated sugar

Preheat the oven to 350 degrees.

Mix all the dry ingredients together except the sugar and set aside. Cream the butter and sugar together. Then beat in the egg and molasses, and add to the dry ingredients and mix well. Form balls 1 inch in diameter, roll them in extra-fine granulated sugar, and place them on an ungreased cookie sheet. Bake 12 to 15 minutes.

Makes approximately 4 dozen cookies

*Alternate recipe to Peanut Butter Cookies

GAME PLAN

The one thing that you can definitely make several days in advance is the cookies. These may even be made weeks in advance and stored in the freezer. The ice is best if made only an hour or so before you intend to serve it, as it can freeze too solid and then you'll have to break it up.

An hour before your guests are due, make the purée and set it in a double boiler, to be warmed later—which will simply involve turning on the heat under it and letting it come to the right temperature slowly.

While the oven is preheating for the monkfish, cook the rice and pasta dish. Put the fish in when this is done. The rice-pasta can wait with a dish towel over it until the fish is cooked—about 10 minutes, depending on its thickness.

Sometime along the way, put the cucumbers, tossed with the mint, on individual plates. You will spoon the dressing over them at the table. If you don't want to use individual plates, toss the cucumbers and dressing together at the very last moment. The salad tends to get watery if this is done too much in advance.

Frank McIntosh European silverplate flatware, salt and pepper shakers (page 106), and heavy glass goblet; Sointu gray crackleware plate; Frank McIntosh random-striped pink-and-white linen napkin.

My Best
Roast Pork
Dinner

I am especially fond of roast pork, but I seem seldom to eat it anymore. So when I do decide to serve it, I want it to be prepared the best and simplest way I know how. This particular method of cooking a boneless loin of pork results in a very moist texture and delicious gravy. To go with the pork is a combination of onions and apples, puréed, that I think is a perfect balance of flavors.

There are also small new potatoes cooked in a cayenne liquid, and steamed squash and sweet green peppers topped w.th balsamic vinegar butter.

For dessert, pears that have been simmered in sweetened strong coffee and topped with chocolate whipped cream.

MENU

Pork Roasted in Milk
Onion-Apple Sauce
Spicy Boiled New Potatoes
Squash and Sweet Green Peppers with
Balsamic Vinegar Butter
Coffee-Poached Pears with Chocolate
Whipped Cream
Wine
Coffee

Above: *Roast pork garnished with thyme,*
new potatoes, and squash and green peppers
Left: *Squash and green peppers ready for serving*
Right: *Coffee-poached pears topped*
with chocolate whipped cream

PORK ROASTED IN MILK

Pork was a favorite in our family when I was a child. However, over the years as I have become more diet- and cholesterol-conscious, I've tended to serve it less. The good thing about this self-imposed restriction is that when I do have it, it is a great treat.

 One 3½-pound loin of pork, boned
3 large garlic cloves, crushed
1 teaspoon dried thyme
 Few drops of Tabasco sauce
 Flour
2 tablespoons safflower oil
2 tablespoons (¼ stick) unsalted butter
1 quart milk, heated
2 bay leaves

Preheat the oven to 325 degrees.

Smear the pork with the crushed garlic and sprinkle on the thyme and Tabasco sauce. Dust very lightly with flour.

In a heavy pot with a lid, heat the oil and butter together. Sear the meat carefully on all sides. Do not have the heat so high that you burn the butter. When it is browned, pour out the oil and add the heated milk and bay leaves. Insert a meat thermometer in the pork and place it in the oven with the lid slightly ajar. Bake for an hour.

Turn up the heat to 375 degrees and remove the lid. Continue to cook for another 45 minutes or more, until the thermometer registers approximately 180 degrees.

When the pork is done, remove it from the cooking liquid—which should be considerably reduced—and skim the fat from the milk. You may boil it down for a few minutes. And since the milk will have curdled, you should either put it through a fine sieve or give it a few whirls in a food processor to smooth it out. It will still be very liquid, but tasty. Correct the seasoning if necessary—but it shouldn't be.

Serves 6 to 8

ONION-APPLE SAUCE

The sweet onions and apples blend marvelously in this sauce. I much prefer it to the more conventional applesauce or apple-horseradish sauce.

This may be made in advance, but if you must refrigerate it, it should be reheated so that it can be served just warm.

2 tablespoons (¼ stick) unsalted butter
3 cups coarsely chopped onions
4 generous cups Granny Smith apple chunks (peel and core the apples)
½ cup tightly packed light brown sugar
 Pinch of salt
1 tablespoon port

Melt the butter in a large skillet (preferably a nonstick) and stir in the onions. Simmer, covered, over very low heat for 10 minutes. Be careful not to scorch them or let them brown. Add the apples, sugar, and salt. Mix. Simmer, covered, for an additional 20 minutes. By this time there should be a good bit of juice and the apples should be tender. If not, cook for a few more minutes. Add the port and boil out most of the liquid at high heat.

In a food processor, purée briefly to a coarse texture.

Makes 3½ cups

SPICY BOILED NEW POTATOES

Often when shrimp or crabs are boiled in that potent mix of herbs and spices favored along the Gulf Coast, small red new potatoes are added to the pot. Cooked this way, potatoes have a delicious bite.

1 large garlic clove, crushed
 Several large shallots, peeled and cut in half
1 small onion, peeled and cut in half
½ large lemon, cut in half
2 large bay leaves, broken into pieces
1 teaspoon cayenne pepper
1 tablespoon crushed black peppercorns
1 teaspoon mustard seeds
1 teaspoon celery seeds
½ teaspoon dried dill
½ teaspoon ground allspice
½ teaspoon ground nutmeg
10 whole cloves
 Salt to taste
2 pounds new potatoes
1 to 2 tablespoons unsalted butter

Pour water into a pot that will accommodate the potatoes snugly. Put in all the ingredients except the potatoes and butter. Bring to a boil. Cover and simmer for 5 to 10 minutes. Add the potatoes (and more water if necessary to cover). Return to a boil and turn the heat down to a simmer. Cook, uncovered, for 15 minutes or until the potatoes are done. Do not undercook.

Drain and toss with butter. Serve hot.

Serves 6

SQUASH AND SWEET GREEN PEPPERS WITH BALSAMIC VINEGAR BUTTER

You may buy any variety of squash except the sweet winter ones, such as acorn squash, for this.
Balsamic vinegar butter is good on almost any vegetable, so remember it.

      Approximately 3 cups sliced or cubed squash, peeled if necessary
2 large sweet green peppers, seeded and cut into thin strips

Balsamic Vinegar Butter
2 tablespoons (¼ stick) unsalted butter or 1 tablespoon each butter and margarine, softened
1½ teaspoons balsamic vinegar
      Salt to taste
      Dash of white pepper (optional)

Put the squash and peppers in a steamer. Steam for approximately 6 minutes, or until the degree of doneness desired. Do not overcook.

Meanwhile, blend the butter and vinegar.

Drain the vegetables and toss with the vinegar butter, salt, and a dash of white pepper if you like.

Serves 6

COFFEE-POACHED PEARS WITH CHOCOLATE WHIPPED CREAM

I am becoming increasingly fond of poached fruit, and the more I experiment with it, the more things I can find to poach it in. Try a little experimenting yourself.

3 large ripe but firm pears, peeled and cored
      Juice of 1 lemon
3 cups strong coffee

Chocolate Whipped Cream
1 ounce unsweetened chocolate, coarsely chopped
4 tablespoons sugar
1 cup heavy cream

Cut pears in half and rub with lemon juice.

In a small saucepan, combine the coffee and sugar and heat. Add the pears. The liquid should just cover them. If not, add a little more coffee (two parts coffee to one part sugar). Simmer 15 minutes, until tender. Remove the pears with a slotted spoon and place in a bowl. Reduce the liquid by three quarters and let cool.

Pour it over the pears and refrigerate.

A little before you are ready to serve, put the chocolate, sugar, and 2 tablespoons of cream in the top of a double boiler. When the chocolate is melted, whip until cooled and set aside. Whisk the rest of the cream and add it to the chocolate.

Place each pear half on a slick of coffee syrup and top with the cream. Garnish with ginger strips.

Serves 6

GAME PLAN

To prepare this meal, start by poaching the pears. This may be done well in advance. You might even do the chocolate for the whipped cream, but not so soon that you feel you will have to refrigerate it.

Next, do the apple and onion sauce. This too may be done pretty well in advance, but not so you will have to refrigerate it either. You may cut up the squash and peppers and cover them with water.

The cooking time for the pork can be slightly uncertain, so count on a good 2 hours before you can serve it. I would also finish the vegetables after the pork is done, not before. Have them ready so you will just have to turn on the heat under the pan when the meat comes out of the oven.

While the vegetables are cooking the meat will wait in a warm spot. You should let meat set for about 10 minutes before slicing it, anyway. This will give you time to finish the sauce and get the rest of the dinner properly organized.

Wolfman-Gold stainless steel flatware; D. F. Sanders all-purpose wineglass; Wedgwood drabware porcelain plate; Frank McIntosh pink linen napkin; antique silver salt and pepper shakers (page 110).

Vegetable Purées

Pear and kohlrabi purée

Unfortunately, foods run in fads, like everything else these days. For a while it was plain basil, and then basil was out; then pesto, and then that was out. Long ago it was quiche, and then quiche went way out—and on and on.

Now, I'm afraid, it is time for purées to be heading for rough sledding. They were so popular right after food processors, with their speedy whirling blades, hit the scene that everything in sight seemed to be puréed. It was good-bye to tedious food mills—and I guess we overdid it.

Be that as it may, purées are a marvelous aid to entertaining, mainly because they provide us with a way to serve tasty fresh vegetables without having to steam them at the last minute to ensure their flavor. Purées can be made hours in advance and left to sit on the stove in a double boiler, to be heated when they are needed. And the flavor and texture are none the worse for the wait. So instead of abandoning them, we should be making new combinations and taking advantage of the convenience they have to offer.

Almost any vegetable can be puréed. Those here are only a few examples for you to begin with. There is really no trick to this except in the seasoning, for which you can trust your own taste and preferences. I have found that one of my favorites, oven-roasted onions, can make a marvelous base for many variations, both sweet and savory. And while you are roasting onions, roast a few big cloves of garlic. To roast onions and garlic, put them in a foil-lined pan and bake, uncovered, in a preheated 425-degree oven until they give when you squeeze them. Onions take 1 to 1¼ hours, garlic only about 25 minutes.

Fourteen recipes are for ordinary nonstarchy vegetables. The other is for a potato and vegetable combination. Many things combine well with potatoes, and since their cooking time is pretty reliable, you may often prepare such a dish along with whatever else is in the oven. Or, if you are serving a roast, which must have a chance to rest for 10 minutes before carving, the timing works out neatly.

Incidentally, all weights here are for cooked vegetables, or peeled and seeded if raw, except where specifically noted. (You will also notice that quantities are measured by weight. This is because it is extremely difficult to accurately measure puréed cooked or coarsely chopped raw vegetables by volume.)

PEAR AND KOHLRABI

1 pound peeled and cubed kohlrabi
½ pound ripe cored and peeled pears
1 tablespoon unsalted butter
Scant ¼ teaspoon white pepper
½ teaspoon fresh lemon juice
1 teaspoon salt, or to taste
Few grinds of nutmeg

Simmer the kohlrabi in lightly salted water for 18 minutes, until fork-tender. Drain. Cut the pears into quarters and steam for 3 minutes. Put everything in a food processor and purée. Correct the seasoning if necessary.

Serves 6

LEEKS AND WAX BEANS

1¼ pounds cleaned leeks (white part only), carefully washed and chopped into ½-inch slices
1¼ pounds wax beans, ends and stems removed
1 teaspoon raspberry vinegar
1 tablespoon plus 1 teaspoon unsalted butter
1 teaspoon salt, or to taste
3 tablespoons crème fraîche
½ teaspoon white pepper

Simmer the leeks in lightly salted water for 15 minutes, or until fork-tender. Drain. Simmer the wax beans for 12 minutes, or until fork-tender. Drain. Put everything in a food processor and purée. Correct the seasoning if necessary.

Serves 6

CARROTS AND CAULIFLOWER

1 pound plus carrots, peeled and cut into thin rings
½ pound cauliflower florets
3 tablespoons unsalted butter
1 teaspoon sherry vinegar
3 tablespoons milk
½ teaspoon salt
Grind of nutmeg

Put the vegetables in the top of a steamer and steam for 6 minutes, until tender. Put them in a food processor, along with the rest of the ingredients. Purée until smooth, scraping down the sides of the bowl as needed. Correct the seasoning, if necessary.

Serves 6

ROASTED ONION AND CAULIFLOWER

1¼ pounds cauliflower, separated into florets
    Milk
1¼ pounds roasted onion (see page 121)
  6 ounces peeled and cored pear
  1 tablespoon plus 1 teaspoon fresh lemon juice
  1 teaspoon salt
  3 tablespoons crème fraîche
    Few grinds of black pepper

Cover the cauliflower with milk and simmer gently for 10 minutes, until fork-tender. Drain. Put everything in a food processor and purée. Correct the seasoning if necessary.

Serves 6

YELLOW AND GREEN SQUASH AND ROASTED ONION

1¼ pounds mixed yellow and green squash, cut into ½-inch rounds
¾ pound roasted onion (see page 121)
 1 tablespoon plus 1 teaspoon unsalted butter
¾ teaspoon salt
  Generous ¼ teaspoon white pepper
¼ teaspoon ground cumin

Cover the squash with lightly salted water and cook for 6 to 8 minutes, until fork-tender (or steam them). Put everything in a food processor and purée. Correct the seasoning if necessary.

Serves 6

BEETS AND RADISHES

1½ pounds unpeeled beets, stemmed but with roots intact
 4 large garlic cloves
¾ pound red bulb radishes, stemmed, with root cut off
 1 tablespoon plus 1 teaspoon unsalted butter
 1 tablespoon plus 1 teaspoon crème fraîche
 1 teaspoon salt
 1 teaspoon red wine vinegar

Preheat the oven to 425 degrees.
    Line a pan with foil, put in the beets, and loosely cover with foil. Bake for 1 hour or more, until fork-tender. Put the garlic in with beets to roast for the last 25 minutes.
    Simmer the radishes in lightly salted water for 10 minutes, until fork-tender. Drain.
    When the beets are cooked, while they are still hot, cut off the stem end; the skins should slip right off. Put them in a food processor fitted with the steel blade. Make a slit in the skin of the garlic and squeeze the pulp into the beets. Discard the skin. Add the rest of the ingredients and purée. Correct the seasoning if necessary.

Serves 6

BUTTERNUT SQUASH AND LEEKS

1¼ pounds butternut squash
    Butter
½ pound leeks (white part only), cleaned and cut into rounds
 1 tablespoon plus 1 teaspoon crème fraîche
¾ teaspoon salt
¼ teaspoon black pepper
    Few grinds of nutmeg

Preheat the oven to 400 degrees and split the squash. Put a dab of butter in the cavity of each after cleaning out the seeds. Line a pan with foil and bake the squash in their skins, for approximately 1 hour, until fork-tender. Cover the leeks with lightly salted water and simmer for 15 minutes, until tender. Scoop out the squash pulp and put everything in a food processor and purée. Correct the seasoning if necessary.

Serves 6

Above: *Carrot and broccoli purée*. Below: *Butternut squash and leek purée*

Above: *Acorn squash and green bean purée.* Below: *Yellow and green squash with roasted onion purée*

CARROTS AND BROCCOLI

1¼ pounds carrots, scraped and cut into
    ½–inch rings
½ pound broccoli florets (tender part only)
2 large garlic cloves
1¼ pounds roasted onion (see page 121)
1 teaspoon balsamic vinegar
1 teaspoon salt
2 tablespoons (¼ stick) unsalted butter
1 tablespoon crème fraîche
    Few grinds of black pepper

Simmer the carrots in lightly salted water for 10 minutes, until fork-tender. Drain. Do the same with the broccoli. Put everything in a food processor and purée. Correct the seasoning if necessary.

Serves 6

ACORN SQUASH AND GREEN BEANS

1 pound acorn squash, halved
¾ pound green beans, ends and stems snapped off
3 tablespoons unsalted butter
1 teaspoon salt
2 teaspoons sugar
    Sprinkling of ground cinnamon
    Scant ¼ teaspoon black pepper

Preheat the oven to 400 degrees.
    Line a pan with foil and place squash in it. Bake for 1 hour, until fork-tender.
    Cover the beans with lightly salted water and simmer for 12 minutes, until fork-tender.
    Put everything in a food processor and purée. Correct the seasoning if necessary.

Serves 6

GREEN PEAS AND FENNEL WITH MINT

1 pound fresh shelled green peas
6 fresh medium-size mint leaves
¾ pound fennel, tender parts only (no leaves or core)
½ teaspoon salt
1 tablespoon plus 2 teaspoons crème fraîche

Simmer the peas and mint leaves in lightly salted water to just cover for 5 minutes, or until tender. Do not overcook. Drain and place in a food processor.
    Coarsely chop the fennel and simmer for 4 minutes, or until tender. The length of time here will depend on how fresh the fennel is. Drain and add to the peas and mint. Add the salt and crème fraîche. Purée. Correct the seasoning if necessary.

Serves 6

POTATOES WITH GREEN ONIONS

3 pounds white potatoes, peeled and cut into cubes
1 cup finely chopped green onion, some green, loosely packed
1 cup milk
1 tablespoon unsalted butter
    Salt and pepper to taste

Place the potatoes in a saucepan and cover with lightly salted water. In the meantime, mix the onions into the milk. Bring just to a simmer. Do not boil. Allow the vegetables to cook for 10 minutes.
    When the potatoes are tender, drain them and return to saucepan. Cover the top with a tea towel. Turn on heat and shake gently to steam some of the moisture out. Incidentally, a tea towel is used here instead of a metal top because you don't want the steam to collect and drip back into the pot. The tea towel will absorb it.
    Add the hot milk-onion mixture and butter to the potatoes. Mash with a hand masher. Add salt and pepper to taste and a little more milk or butter if you like. Do not use a food processor for this as it will make the texture of the potatoes gluey.

Serves 6

RUTABAGA AND APPLES

2 medium Granny Smith apples, approximately ¾ pounds, peeled, cored, and thickly sliced
1½ to 2 pounds rutabagas, peeled and thickly sliced
½ teaspoon salt
2 teaspoons fresh lemon juice
    Few grinds black pepper
    Dash of mace

Steam the apple slices until tender, approximately 2 minutes. Put into a food processor.

Steam the rutabaga slices until tender, approximately 4 minutes. Combine with the apples. Add the salt, lemon juice, pepper, and mace. Purée. Correct the seasoning if necessary.

Serves 6

ROASTED ONION, CAULIFLOWER, AND LEEKS

½ pound leeks (white part only), cleaned and cut into ½–inch rings
¾ pound cauliflower florets
  Milk
1 pound onion, roasted (see page 88)
1 tablespoon plus 1 teaspoon unsalted butter
1 tablespoon plus 1 teaspoon crème fraîche
1 teaspoon salt
1 teaspoon lemon juice
  Few grinds of black pepper

Cover the leeks with lightly salted water and simmer for 15 minutes, until fork-tender. Drain. Cover the cauliflower with milk and simmer for 10 minutes, until fork-tender. Drain.

Put everything in a food processor and purée. Correct the seasoning if necessary.

Serves 6

BRUSSELS SPROUTS, ROASTED SHALLOTS, AND ROASTED YELLOW PEPPERS

2 medium sweet yellow peppers, approximately ½ pound
¾ pound shallots
2 boxes Brussels sprouts, approximately 1½ pounds
½ teaspoon salt
4 teaspoons fresh lemon juice
1 tablespoon plus 2 teaspoons unsalted butter
1 tablespoon crème fraîche
  Dash of white pepper
  Dash of nutmeg

To roast the peppers, first turn the oven up to broil and allow it to preheat. Then place the peppers on a piece of foil under the flame and roast until completely blackened, turning often with tongs. Place blackened peppers in a brown paper bag and fold the top shut to allow them to "sweat." When the peppers are cool, peel and seed them. Turn the oven down to 400 degrees.

Line a small pie pan with foil and place the unpeeled shallots in it. Bake until soft when squeezed, approximately 25 minutes. Set aside to cool slightly.

While the shallots are cooling, trim the Brussels sprouts and steam them until fork-tender. When cooked, place the Brussels sprouts in a food processor.

Peel the shallots by snipping off tops and bottoms with kitchen shears and squeezing out the soft center into the food processor. Add the salt, lemon juice, butter, crème fraîche, pepper, and nutmeg. Purée. Correct the seasoning if necessary.

Serves 6

CARROTS AND BAKED ONIONS

3 pounds large onions (Vidalia, if possible)
3 pounds carrots, scraped and cut into rings
3 tablespoons unsalted butter
1 tablespoon sherry vinegar
2 tablespoons sugar
  Salt to taste

Preheat the oven to 400 degrees.

To roast onions, choose a pan large enough to hold them in a single layer and line it with foil. Place the onions in the pan, put it in the oven, uncovered, and bake for 1 hour and 15 minutes.

In the meantime, cover the carrots with lightly salted water and simmer for about 15 minutes, until fork-tender. You might do this toward the end of the onion cooking time. Drain the carrots and keep warm.

When the onions are done, let cool until you can just handle them and peel off the first couple of layers. The root end will usually come right off, but the stem end often has little tough pieces sticking up. These are difficult to cut off with a knife, so use kitchen shears. Cut the onions in half and put them in a food processor, along with the carrots, butter, vinegar, and sugar. Process until puréed. Add salt and correct the seasoning.

Serves 8

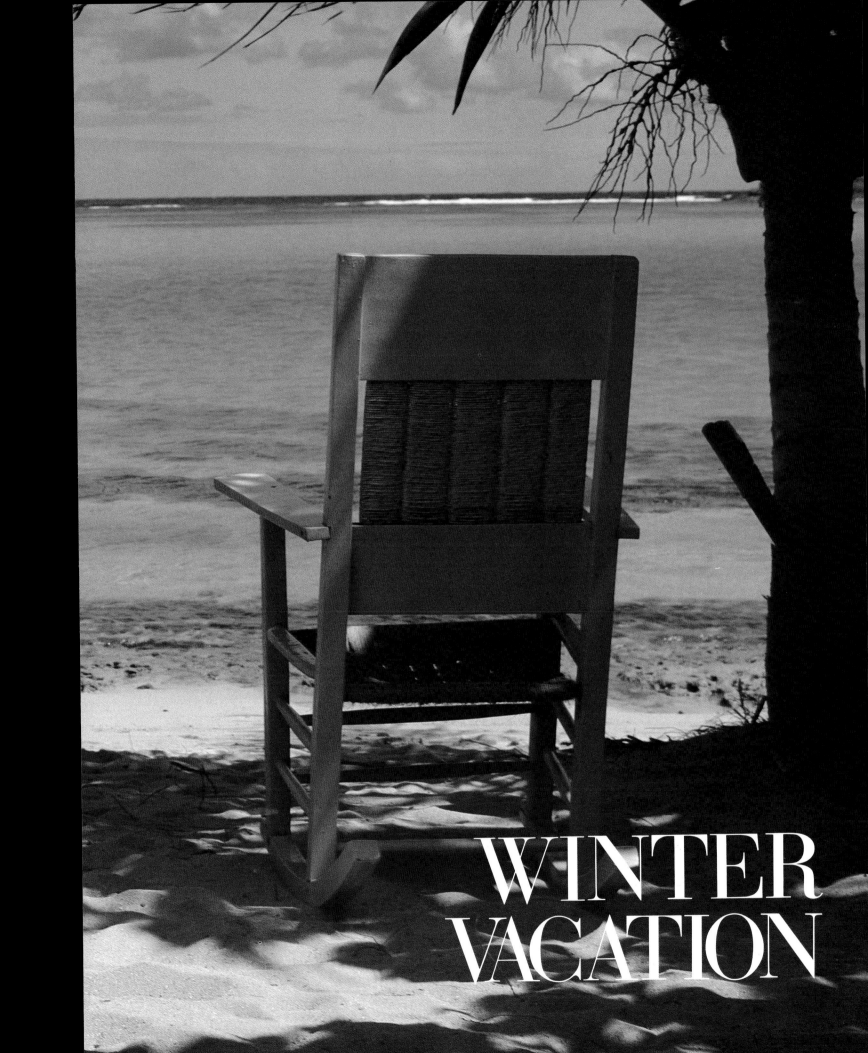

WINTER
VACATION

Winter Vacation

After the swirling excitement of fall in the city and the hectic fun of Christmas and New Year's, bleak winter reality closes in. Dinner conversation will often fix on plans for an escape to where the sun can toast our pale bodies and lift our winter-eroded spirits. Daydreams turn to the prospect of interrupting, with a winter vacation, the long frigid slide toward spring. A quick getaway is in order. So it is that in mid-February I will frequently find myself with a bunch of friends who have banded together and rented a house on some Caribbean island. For the past few years now, that island has been St. Barths. While there, about half the time we take our meals at home. And on St. Barths, like most other islands in the area, eating at home means we are presented with the challenge of planning menus and cooking under less than ideal conditions. Most of the kitchens on the island are large but not particularly well equipped— by our spoiled city standards, at least—and you never know from one day to the next what foodstuffs you will find in the markets. There are times when it seems all their shelves can offer up are restaurant-size tins of black pepper and shriveled cucumbers. But we soon learn to make do as

we get into the rhythm of the place, planning carefully enough to go where we are most likely to find what we want—and remembering to be flexible enough to accept changed plans when main ingredients counted on are simply not to be found. So it is St. Barths, with its sometimes charming limitations and surprising bounty, which is the inspiration for the following recipes and combinations of foods. A little lesson about rolling with the prevailing tide when you are cooking and planning under unfamiliar and limited circumstances is probably in there someplace.

Because St. Barths is a French island, very good local bread, dry sausages and salami, and cheeses are to be found—as well as "exotic" staples such as crème fraîche. However, often we will be stopped by puzzling gaps like the lack of dried basil or canned anchovies. We solve this by having friends bring down the anchovies, and I throw in a can of basil when I am packing. But, strangest of all, there is very little fresh fish, except in restaurants. I can live with any of these minor lapses because St. Barths has one of the most wonderful (to me) food assets going: a constant supply of fresh tomatoes, which I understand are shipped in from some of the larger vegetable-producing spots, like St. Thomas. Wherever they come from, they are almost worth the trip south—in case you are looking for a reason. So we eat sliced tomatoes as part of most meals; when not sliced, they usually find their way into whatever main dish we make. This marvelous tomato gluttony makes going back to New York City and those terrible (not to mention expensive) ersatz substitutes we have to put up with during the cold months almost unbearable.

I became acquainted with a French terrine dish in St. Barths that I had been aware of for years, but had seldom eaten, called "rillettes." It is a sort of pork pâté and is absolutely mouth-watering. And since pork is so popular where I hail from originally, I took to it immediately. It is just right at lunch, munched along with sour cornichon pickles (always available) and crusty bread with butter, black olives, and those grand tomatoes. To top it off, wine is good and cheap. Incidentally, we buy the rillettes already prepared, but I have learned to make it and so I've included the recipe.

Because the quality of the meat tends to vary, we use it sparingly, mostly at dinner. And thank heavens for pasta. Since it

can be sauced with practically anything, and rates as one of almost everyone's favorites, pasta makes an ideal island meal. All you have to do is follow it with local fruit for dessert.

As a matter of fact, the very limitations that one has to live with in the islands, where you don't have every possible ingredient at your fingertips, can create their own moments of sharpened pleasure. As when suddenly, out of nowhere, a treasured but elusive ingredient miraculously appears in the local market. Or when someone arrives from home bearing an incredible luxury—such as a big chunk of Parmesan cheese, good-quality Parmesan never being available in any of the markets. Under such circumstances, food like this, which we take for granted most of the time, can assume the importance of a great treat. Who needs crème fraîche, chèvre, cornichons, foie gras, inexpensive good champagne, and the like when you can have Parmesan toast!

So it is out to the markets early, with an open mind and your ingenuity at the ready, to see what you can rustle up. Then on to another sun-filled day.

Above: *Pasta shells with tuna and tomato sauce.* Below: *Fettuccine with tomato and bacon sauce*

Rillettes with bread and garnishes

FETTUCCINE WITH HOT TOMATO AND BACON SAUCE

I've made this pasta almost everywhere we have gone for a vacation. The necessary ingredients are almost always available in one form or another.

If there are no fresh tomatoes, substitute a large can (approximately 2 pounds plus) of tomatoes, drained and chopped.

This sauce also keeps quite well.

- ½ pound thick bacon slices
- 3 tablespoons olive oil
- 2½ large onions, chopped
- 3 garlic cloves, crushed
- 5 large tomatoes (about 3 pounds) peeled, seeded, and chopped
- 1 tablespoon salt
- 1 tablespoon dried tarragon
- ¼ teaspoon red pepper flakes or cayenne pepper
- 1 teaspoon black pepper
- 4 tablespoons finely chopped fresh parsley
- 1 pound fettuccine
    Unsalted butter
    Grated Parmesan cheese

Fry the bacon until crisp, drain on paper towels, and set aside. Pour out all the fat except for 1 tablespoon. Add the olive oil to this, and when hot, add the onions. Wilt (about 5 minutes) and add the garlic and tomatoes. Simmer for a few minutes, then add the salt, tarragon, and red and black pepper. Simmer for another half hour, stirring occasionally. Add the parsley. Simmer for 5 minutes. Crumble the bacon and stir it in. The sauce may be used now or reheated later.

To serve, cook the pasta in a large quantity of boiling water until al dente. Drain. Put it back in the pot and toss with a little butter. Mix with some of the sauce and pass the rest. Top each serving with freshly grated Parmesan cheese.

Serves 6

RUSTIC SALAD

This is called by many different names in restaurants in St. Barths. I have chosen the name "Rustic" just because it was the first one to come to mind. It is always a great hit with guests, served with Parmesan toast and followed by a big fruit dessert.

- 12 thick bacon slices
- 2 tablespoons safflower oil
- 2 tablespoons finely minced onion
- 2 tablespoons red wine vinegar
- ¼ teaspoon salt
- ½ teaspoon black pepper
- 1½ cups large cubes of French bread
- 3 tablespoons olive oil
- 3 heads romaine lettuce, washed, dried, and torn into pieces
- 6 eggs

Cut the bacon into ½-inch pieces and fry until crisp. Set aside to drain on paper towels. Reserve 3 tablespoons of the bacon fat, add the safflower oil to it, and heat. Sauté the onion until golden. Add the vinegar, salt, and pepper. Set aside on the stove.

Put the bread cubes on a cookie sheet and toast in the oven. When golden, heat the olive oil and fry them. Set aside.

To serve, toss together the croutons, bacon, and lettuce. Add just enough dressing to lightly coat the lettuce leaves. Put on large individual plates and set aside.

Poach the eggs in a large shallow pan of simmering water by breaking individual eggs into a saucer and sliding each into the water. Carefully remove the eggs with a slotted spoon, blot to dry, and place on top of the salads. Spoon a little of the dressing over the eggs and pass the rest.

Serves 6

PASTA SHELLS WITH UNCOOKED TUNA AND TOMATO SAUCE

It is always good to have a dish that can be made when the weather is too hot to stay in the kitchen long. This fills the bill and is a delightful change.

If you are not too keen on anchovies, reduce the amount called for by half or even more. But don't leave them out all together, as they are an important element. You might also mix in 3 or 4 coarsely grated hard-boiled eggs just before serving, if you like.

1 can (6½ ounces) Italian tuna in olive oil, drained
1 can flat anchovies, drained and chopped
½ cup black olives in oil, pitted and chopped
5 tablespoons basil olive oil*
2 tablespoons safflower oil
1 tablespoon fresh lemon juice
4 tablespoons finely chopped fresh parsley
3 medium garlic cloves, mashed and finely chopped
1 large bunch green onions (with some top), finely chopped
1 pound pasta shells
2 medium tomatoes, coarsely chopped

Break up the tuna into small pieces and add all the remaining ingredients except the pasta and tomatoes. Mix thoroughly and cover. Refrigerate overnight.

To serve, let the sauce come to room temperature and cook the shells in a large quantity of salted water. Toss the shells with the sauce and sprinkle with chopped tomatoes, or pass the tomatoes separately.

Serves 6

*Put 2 teaspoons dried basil in 5 tablespoons olive oil and let it marinate for several days.

GREEN SALAD WITH TOASTED GOAT CHEESE (CHÈVRE)

I like the salad greens for this to be as simple as possible—Boston lettuce is my preference, but any mild lettuce would do. You could add other ingredients if you choose, but I don't think they are necessary.

Lettuce, washed, dried, and torn into bits
½ teaspoon salt
¼ teaspoon black pepper
1 generous teaspoon Dijon mustard
2 tablespoons red wine vinegar
3 tablespoons safflower oil
2 tablespoons olive oil
12 thick slices mild goat cheese
Twelve ½-inch slices French bread

Put the lettuce in a bowl and refrigerate, covered. Meanwhile, make the salad dressing by combining the salt, pepper, mustard, and vinegar. Mix well. Whisk in the oils. Set aside, unrefrigerated.

Put slices of cheese on the French bread slices and toast under the broiler. While this is toasting, toss the dressing with the lettuce and divide among 6 individual plates. Serve with toasted cheese bread on the plate.

Serves 6

WHITE BEAN WITH TUNA SALAD

Bean salads are marvelous in the warm weather, either as part of a larger meal or as a meal in themselves. They may be as simple as white beans tossed with olive oil, a grind of black pepper, and a squeeze of lemon, or they may have as many more ingredients as you like. I really have no preference, making it one way one time and another the next.

1 pound dried white beans
1 large onion, peeled and cut in half
Salt to taste
Pepper to taste
¼ cup good-quality olive oil, or more to taste
1 can Italian tuna in oil, drained
1 small green pepper, finely chopped
1 small red onion, finely chopped
Juice of ½ small lemon

Garnish
Lemon wedges

Cover the beans with water and soak them overnight. (Or cover with water, bring to a boil, turn the heat down to a simmer, and cook for 3 minutes. Turn off the heat and let them sit in the water for 1 hour.) Drain the beans and add the halved onion. Cover with water to about an inch above beans. Add salt and pepper. Simmer until tender. The time will vary according to the age of the beans.

Pour off any excess liquid and let cool for a few minutes. Pour the olive oil over the beans and toss lightly. Let cook completely and add all the remaining ingredients, and more oil if you like. Correct the seasoning.

Serve with wedges of lemon.

Serves 6 to 8

Above: *Chicken cutlets, Parmesan toast, leeks, tomatoes, onions, and peppers.* Below: *Green salad with toasted goat cheese*

Above: *Rustic salad.* Below: *White bean and tuna salad, lentil salad, rice salad*

LENTIL SALAD

These lentils could be turned into a very good, very easy soup with the addition of more chicken stock.

1 pound dried brown lentils
1 large onion, chopped
2 large shallots, chopped
    Chicken stock, heated
4 to 6 drops Tabasco sauce
2 tablespoons good quality olive oil
½ cup finely chopped celery (with some tender yellow leaves)
    Salt and pepper to taste

Cover the lentils with boiling water to about an inch above them. Let sit for 1½ hours. Drain and put in a pot with the onion and shallots. Add the chicken stock and bring just to a simmer. Cook very gently for about 10 minutes, until just tender, adding more stock if necessary. Do not overcook. Stir the Tabasco sauce into the olive oil and mix into the lentils. Let cool.

To serve, mix in the celery and correct the seasoning.

Serves 6 to 8

RICE SALAD

Like the other salads, this may have as many ingredients as strike your fancy. Also, it may have as much dressing as you like. Some people like it very soupy and others don't.

The only thing to know about this salad is that it does not last very well in the refrigerator, so just make what you will serve at one sitting. It isn't that the salad spoils, but the texture of the rice and the overall flavor deteriorate in 5 to 6 hours.

1 cup raw rice
2 cups chicken stock
¾ cup fresh or canned green peas, drained
1 medium sweet red pepper, roasted (see page 121), peeled, seeded, and cut into strips or dice
3 large green onions (with some top), chopped into medium rings
1 generous tablespoon small capers
2 generous tablespoons chopped sweet pickle
2 tablespoons chopped chives
2 tablespoons chopped fresh dill
½ teaspoon salt
¼ teaspoon black pepper
1 teaspoon Dijon mustard
2 tablespoons red wine vinegar
3 tablespoons safflower oil
2 tablespoons olive oil
2 generous tablespoons mayonnaise

Garnish
    Additional roasted red pepper strips

Cover the rice with chicken stock in a small pan. Bring to a boil. Simmer for 10 minutes (do not let it overflow), stirring occasionally. Test for doneness. If not done, let it cook for another minute or two. Rinse with very hot water, drain, and set aside. You may do this several hours in advance.

When ready to serve, fluff up the rice and toss in the peas, red pepper, green onions, capers, pickle, chives, and dill. Set aside.

Mix the salt, pepper, mustard, and vinegar. Whisk in the oils. Stir in the mayonnaise, mixing well. Toss into the salad. Correct the seasoning if necessary. Garnish with strips of pepper.

Serves 6

RILLETTES

This is the pâtélike concoction I love. I make it from a recipe given to me by Susan Costner and included in her book Gifts of Food.

1¼ pounds lean pork, cut into cubes
¾ pound pork fat, diced, and ½ pound country-style bacon, diced (or any combination of fat and bacon totaling 1¼ pounds)
¼ teaspoon salt
    Coarsely ground black pepper to taste
    Pinch of nutmeg
1 teaspoon herbes de Provence
½ teaspoon fresh thyme
1 teaspoon juniper berries
1 teaspoon coriander seeds
3 or 4 shallots, cut in half
1 bay leaf
1 garlic clove
6 to 8 parsley sprigs
½ cup water
¼ cup Cognac
    Bay leaves for decoration

Preheat the oven to 325 degrees.

Put the pork, pork fat, and bacon in a large mixing bowl. Add the salt, pepper, nutmeg, herbes de Provence, and thyme. Toss together and put the mixture in a deep enameled casserole.

Tie the juniper berries, coriander seeds, shallots, bay leaf, garlic, and parsley in a square of cheesecloth with a string attached for easy removal. Add this bouquet garni, the water, and the Cognac to the casserole and bring to a boil on top of the stove.

Cover the casserole and bake in the oven for 3½ to 4 hours. Remove the bouquet garni after 3 hours. The liquid will evaporate and the meat should brown slightly. If the meat browns too quickly, reduce the heat to 300 degrees.

Transfer the meat to a strainer lined with cheesecloth, set over a large bowl to catch the fat. Reserve the fat.

After the meat has cooled, shred it either with your hands or with two forks. Put the meat in a 4- to 5-cup earthenware container, or divide it between several small ramekins. Press down to compress the meat slightly, but do not pack it too tightly. Use three quarters of the reserved fat to cover the rillettes so that no meat is exposed to the air. Cover and refrigerate until the fat is set.

Remove the rillettes from the refrigerator and make an additional thin layer with the remaining fat. If there is not enough fat left from the cooking, render additional pork or bacon or use melted lard. Gently press the bay leaves into a pattern on top of the fat and refrigerate until hard. Sealed with the fat, this will keep for several months in the refrigerator.

Makes 4 cups

CHICKEN CUTLETS, PARMESAN TOAST AND LEEK VINAIGRETTE WITH RED ONION

Chicken cutlets are best served at room temperature and require just a squeeze of lemon to pique their flavor. A perfect lunch dish. (Do not refrigerate unless absolutely necessary.) The method of preparation is quite simple and is essentially the same as the one used to cook the sliced turkey breast on page 92. Here boned chicken breasts, which should be flattened slightly between two sheets of waxed paper before starting, are used instead of the turkey.

To make Parmesan toast, generously butter medium to thin slices of French bread and sprinkle with freshly grated Parmesan cheese. These may either be toasted in the oven, which makes the bread crisper, or run under the broiler. I prefer the bread fairly thin and toasted in the oven.

Prepare leeks vinaigrette by first poaching them slowly in a good rich chicken stock—making sure they are well washed beforehand. When leeks are fork-tender, turn off heat and allow them to cool in the stock, where

they may remain for several hours. To serve, drain, reserving the stock, and cut each in half lengthwise, then place on individual salad plates. Spoon a bit of strong vinaigrette over each and top with finely chopped red onion.

Incidentally, do not discard the poaching stock. It makes a wonderful base for cold tomato or potato soup.

BANANAS IN BROWN SUGAR AND RUM

Most places in New Orleans call this "Bananas Foster." It is a delightful dessert and never tastes as good to me as it does on some island with the gentle breezes blowing. In St. Barths there is a particularly tasty small banana that is perfectly suited to this dish.

Should the sauce get too caramelized, fill the pan with cold water as soon as you pour out the sauce. Otherwise the pan can be the devil to clean.

> 8 tablespoons (1 stick) unsalted butter
> ½ cup tightly packed dark brown sugar
> 6 small bananas, peeled and split in half lengthwise (if the bananas are very small, allow 1½ per person)
> 6 ounces light or dark rum
>   Whipped cream or vanilla ice cream

Put the butter and sugar in a shallow pan. Melt them very slowly and add the bananas. Cook for 2 minutes on each side, until just tender. Turn only once. (Start bananas on their round side—I find them easier to turn that way.) Place on individual plates. Add rum to the pan, swirl around, and bring to a boil. Do not overcook. Pour over the bananas.

Serve with whipped cream or vanilla ice cream.

Serves 6

MIXED TROPICAL FRUIT

There is no recipe for this one. We simply buy whatever looks good in the market that day—watermelon and other melons, pineapple, starfruit, mangos or papaya, in any combination. I am particularly partial to melons, so whatever else there is, I usually start with one.

If you have the inclination, you can make a kind of ice by forcing fruit pulp through a sieve and adding sugar and a bit of lemon juice to taste. Then pour the mixture into metal ice-cube trays (without the dividers), or some other kind of metal container, and freeze, stirring occasionally to keep it from becoming solid.

MY
KITCHEN
AND
TABLE

Pots, Pans, Appliances

It has taken a lot of years and a lot of mistakes to get my kitchen to work the way I want it to. And even then I seem constantly to be thinking of slight changes I would like to make. For instance, although I finally now have enough closet and shelf space, I found that the way I was storing flat things such as cookie sheets, odd-size lids, and even metal pie pans, was not working. As a matter of fact, every time I wanted to pull a seldom-used something out, I created a waterfall of clattering metal, followed by a stream of unprintables from me. This winter I have finally gotten around to having the carpenter put in slots to keep me sane.

I suppose the thing to do is be calm and enjoy the process. Not easy for me. My continuing interest in experimenting with new (to me) ingredients, dishes, and ways of preparing food invariably requires some special equipment. Then what to do with it? As you can imagine, this only aggravates the storage problem. That and the fact that I'm so reluctant to throw away anything to do with the kitchen which, incidentally, runs counter to my usual behavior. In every other situation I really do believe in Ludwig Mies van der Rohe's maxim about less being more, and regularly get rid of things I don't use.

In common with almost all other cooks, I have special pots, pans, knives, and gadgets that I am partial to. Some of them are not even as efficient as they might be, or as nice-looking as my designer eye wants, but are too dear—for God knows what reason—to replace. A typical example is a bent metal measuring cup that I retrieved about twenty-five years ago when my aunt was throwing it out. Originally I wanted it to melt chocolate in. My chocolate-melting days are few now, but the cup remains, and I'd hate to be without it.

Such quirks and other foolishness aside, there is basic equipment that one should invest in to make the kitchen efficient and easy—things that you use on a more or less regular basis, like a certain number of pots and knives, skillets and pans, etc. So read about equipping a kitchen in one of the good cooking reference books, like *The Joy of Cooking*, my bible from the beginning. This will help give you a plan from which to build. You don't have to have everything right off, but at least the list will guide you when faced with the welter of choices available in housewares. Once you have your basics in place, let your enthusiasms and interests tell you what you need—just as it has done with me.

In this following section you will see pictures of the equipment I use. Design means a lot to me and in at least one case takes precedence over function, as with the elegant Opa pots and lids I was using even before they were available in the United States. Their finish and design were so beautiful to me, and the placement of the matching handles on both tops and lids were so pleasing, I couldn't resist. The problem is with these very handles. Because there is one on each side of the lid instead of a single grip on top, two hands, instead of one, are needed to lift it off easily. Of course, it can be argued that this side placement allows the pots to be stacked. Whatever, I wouldn't want to change my choice.

And I suppose a reasonable argument could be made against old-fashioned black cast iron skillets, because they are a pain in the neck to cure and maintain. But for making certain things they just can't seem to be beat. And for me they have very strong and pleasant memory associations.

As your kitchen grows and your cooking preferences become more evident to you, you'll find that one of the best investments you can make is in equipment of the proper size and shape. The right pot for the right job can make all the difference in the world.

I mentioned earlier that I don't like to jettison any of my unused kitchen equipment. This is not just the pack rat in me coming out, but because my interest in certain foods seems to burn hot for a while and then wane. But I've been cooking long enough now to know that if you wait, this enthusiasm will be revived and the neglected special supplies pressed back into service.

I suppose one of the best purchases I have made for the kitchen over the years was a stove with two ovens. That second oven sure does come in handy, as do the extra burners on top.

Anyway, putting a well-stocked kitchen together is a pleasure. It can take years—and should. So try to enjoy the doing.

SOURCES FOR THE FOLLOWING PAGES:
1. Calphalon 12" saucepan with cover at Dean & Deluca, 121 Prince Street, New York, NY 10012.
2. Stainless steel mixing bowls at Dean & Deluca, 121 Prince Street, New York, NY 10012.
3. Aluminum pasta pot with takeout colander plus separate rice steamer by Leyse at Lee Bailey at Henri Bendel, 10 West 57th Street, New York, NY 10019.
4. Stainless steel all-purpose pots by Opa (made in Denmark) at Lee Bailey at Henri Bendel, 10 West 57th Street, New York, NY 10019.
5. Stainless steel teapot by Cuisinart at Lee Bailey at Henri Bendel, 10 West 57th Street, New York, NY 10019.
6. Grooved carving board and cook's knives by Wusthof Trident, both at Dean & Deluca, 121 Prince Street, New York, NY 10012. Individual French pepper grinder at Lee Bailey at Henri Bendel, 10 West 57th Street, New York, NY 10019.
7. French white porcelain soufflé dishes by Pillivyt and clear glass soufflé dishes by American Laboratory, both at Dean & Deluca, 121 Prince Street, New York, NY 10012.
8. Silverstone nonstick aluminum skillets by Leyse at W. G. Lemmon Ltd., 755 Madison Avenue, New York, NY 10021.
9. Mini espresso/cappuccino machine by Krups at Lee Bailey at Henri Bendel, 10 West 57th Street, New York, NY 10019.
10. Steel deep fryer with removable wire blanching basket at Dean & Deluca, 121 Prince Street, New York, NY 10012.
11. Adjustable wide-mouth toaster by Maxim at Lee Bailey at Henri Bendel, 10 West 57th Street, New York, NY 10019.
12. 10-cup coffee machine by Krups at Lee Bailey at Henri Bendel, 10 West 57th Street, New York, NY 10019.
13. Stainless steel roasting pans at Dean & Deluca, 121 Prince Street, New York, NY 10012.
14. Stainless steel saucepans with copper bottoms by Krona at Lee Bailey at Henri Bendel, 10 West 57th Street, New York, NY 10019.
15. Stainless steel multi-use roaster/steamer/broiler/fish poacher at Lee Bailey at Henri Bendel, 10 West 57th Street, New York, NY 10019.
16. Natural cast-iron skillet and frying pans by Lodge at Dean & Deluca, 121 Prince Street, New York, NY 10012.

9

10

11

12

13

14

15

16

Gadgets

You ou would think that for someone like me, who is involved in the design business and is so interested in food, too, my favorite store would be some beautifully appointed shop selling the latest in functional design, or one of those sublime Italian food markets with their grand and glorious displays. These are pretty high on my list, it's true, but in my heart of hearts, my favorite can be found in almost any town or city. It is the hardware store. I've been haunting them since I was a kid. Something about these places, where I regularly find stuff that tickles my imagination, really gets to me. I always wonder what inspired the clever person who came up with one of these often very simple but ingenious contraptions. Contraptions to pull a nail without bending it, to neatly strip the insulation off wires, to quickly make wooden joints fit and trim, to scour pans with ease, to start fires in a moment (or put them out). It seems endless.

Being barely medium handy with tools myself makes some of these have an almost magical quality. And plenty of good design is there, too, usually of the most honest kind: unadorned tools and devices whose functions dictate their design, as when handles or protrusions reflect the grasp of a hand—the pinch of two fingers. It's only when some stylist someplace decides to do them in "decorator colors" or adds a "decorator design" that the whole thing goes wrong. Whoever came up with the insipid colors "Harvest Gold" and "Avocado Green," not to mention such terrible corny names, should be shot from a cannon.

Well, anyway, having such strong opinions about, and attraction to, hardware stores and the products they sell, it is small wonder that I have a weakness for gadgets—the limited meaning of which is simply "a device or contrivance." That definition's not good enough for me; I like to think of a gadget as a device contrived for a very narrow purpose, which sprang from the logical and inventive mind of some guy who really knows his business.

I think we gadget lovers have gotten a bum rap. Let's face it, people who don't share our enthusiasm take us to be slightly nuts. In all charity, I suppose these unreconstructed types lack the imagination to fantasize about the uses of these glorious devices—poor souls.

On the next pages you will find pictures and sources of some of my favorite kitchen gadgets. They are things that I use all the time, and they really do make cooking easier for me.

One, which is standard in practically all kitchens

these days, is the "old-fashioned" potato peeler. But, old or not, no one has come up with anything to do the job better. Almost as ubiquitous is the garlic press, now in a self-cleaning version. Another favorite of mine: the pull-cord salad spinner, which dries salad greens. What did I do before it came along? Same with the fish measure, which tells you how long to cook the fish by its thickness. Also to make measuring easier is the Pepper-Mate pepper mill, which collects fresh pepper as it is ground.

For my money, one of the greatest gadgets to pop up recently is the triple timer. Lightweight and battery-operated, it allows you to time three things at once. Maybe just because my memory is so rotten, I use it to remind myself to do everything from taking the cake out of the oven to getting back in the kitchen to finish the balance of the dinner so it will all come out together.

Still another gadget I depend on is the hand ricer, primarily for hard-boiled eggs. I am a stickler when it comes to the texture of egg salad (one of my favorite things), and I have found that the ricer does the job best. If the ricer isn't handy I reach for a one-sided grater. This flat version is ideal for small grating jobs, like one egg or a scrap of cheese or part of a lemon—much less cumbersome and more easily washed than the usual four-sided number. And, speaking of lemons, I use a juicer (with a handle) that fits neatly over a measuring cup. It gets the juice out and lets it go directly into the cup while holding back seeds. And it, too, is easy to wash and store—lots better than those big glass ones.

Back to eggs for a minute, I have a thingamabob with a small retractable cup top centered over a sharp point that pierces an egg so that, when boiled, the shell will not adhere to the white. Terrific. I also have a marvelous timer that goes in the pot with the eggs that allows you to boil them to the right degree of doneness. And while we're on the subject of boiling water, did you know there's a device called a "pot watch" that prevents liquid from boiling over when it's put in the pot?

This year I also discovered Magi-Cake strips that, when dampened and pinned around the outside of cake pans before baking, keep the layers level, making them easier to stack and ice.

My current gadget of choice vacuum-seals food in bags for freezing, which can then be put directly in boiling water to thaw. What next?

I can hardly wait for the new year.

SOURCES FOR FOLLOWING PAGES:
1. *Potato ricer at Bridge Kitchen Ware, 214 East 52nd Street, New York, NY 10022.*
2. *Magi-Cake baking strips at Lee Bailey at Henri Bendel, 10 West 57th Street, New York, NY 10019.*
3. *Aluminum juicer at W. G. Lemmon Ltd., 755 Madison Avenue, New York, NY 10021.*
4. *Perfect Fish measure at Lee Bailey at Henri Bendel, 10 West 57th Street, New York, NY 10019.*
5. *Hand grater at Lee Bailey at Henri Bendel, 10 West 57th Street, New York, NY 10019.*
6. *Pastry blender at M. H. Lamston stores across the country.*
7. *The Pepper Mate pepper mill by Easthampton Industries at Lee Bailey at Henri Bendel, 10 West 57th Street, New York, NY 10019.*
8. *Egg piercer at Bridge Kitchen Ware, 214 East 52nd Street, New York, NY 10022.*
9. *Eggrite egg timer by Wahl at Lee Bailey at Henri Bendel, 10 West 57th Street, New York, NY 10019.*
10. *Fresh Lock vacuum sealer by Deni at Lee Bailey at Henri Bendel, 10 West 57th Street, New York, NY 10019.*
11. *Simmer Plate flame diffuser at M. H. Lamston stores across the country.*
12. *Pear/apple corer, zester, and citrus stripper at Lee Bailey at Henri Bendel, 10 West 57th Street, New York, NY 10019.*
13. *Triple Timer by West Bend at Lee Bailey at Henri Bendel, 10 West 57th Street, New York, NY 10019.*
14. *Rotor salad spinner at Lee Bailey at Henri Bendel, 10 West 57th Street, New York, NY 10019.*
15. *Salad dressing shaker at Lee Bailey at Henri Bendel, 10 West 57th Street, New York, NY 10019.*
16. *Stainless steel champagne/wine recorker by Bailey-Bannett Inc. at Lee Bailey at Henri Bendel, 10 West 57th Street, New York, NY 10019.*
17. *Long-reaching basting brush by Sparta at Lee Bailey at Henri Bendel, 10 West 57th Street, New York, NY 10019.*
18. *Jar opener by Kaplan/Aronson at W. G. Lemmon Ltd., 755 Madison Avenue, New York, NY 10021.*
19. *Stainless steel instant meat thermometer by Cuisinart at Lee Bailey at Henri Bendel, 10 West 57th Street, New York, NY 10019.*
20. *Glass pot watch at W. G. Lemmon Ltd., 755 Madison Avenue, New York, NY 10021.*

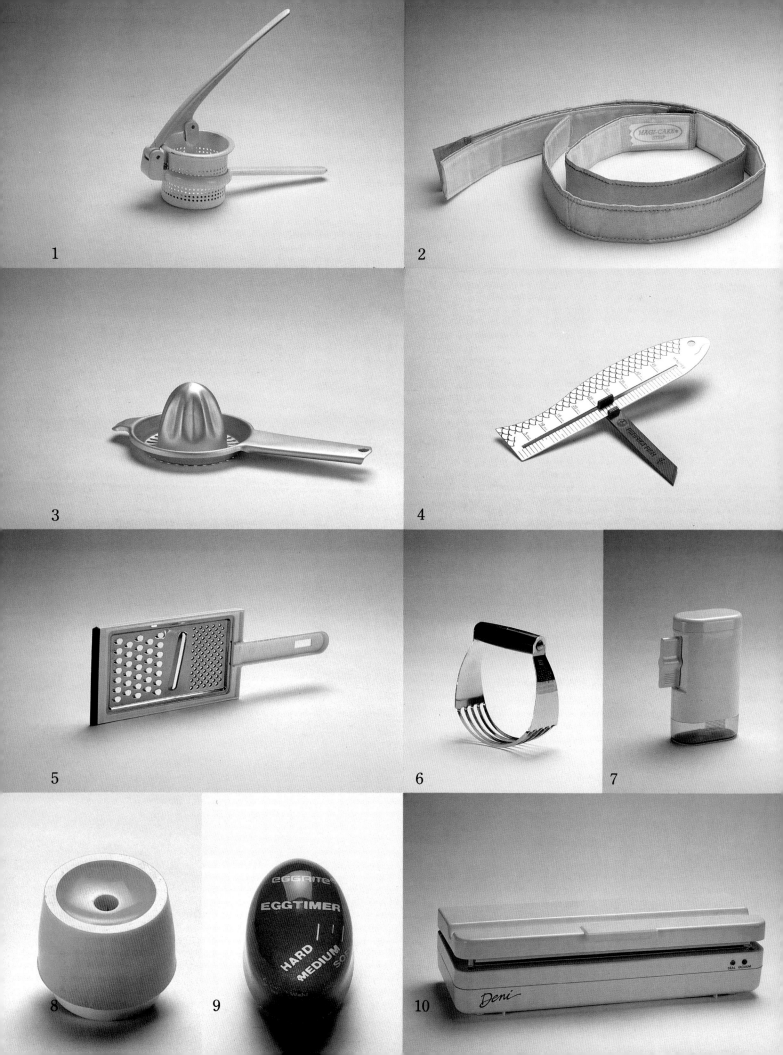

1

2

3

4

5

6

7

8

9

10

11

12

13

14

15

16

17

18

19

20

Plates

My feeling about all plates is that they should not compete with the food. They are the background. Admittedly, such sentiment considerably narrows one's options. But busy patterns and overly bright colors simply make food look less appetizing, to my eye. So I suppose if I had to choose one plate it would be a classic unadorned white of the best-quality porcelain.

This notion started a long time ago—like a majority of other big-city design students of my day, the dinnerware I bought for myself when I set up my first apartment was white "Arzberg." Later came its heartier relative, white "Arabia" ware. Probably most of us then were moved to make this choice because the simplicity of these dishes was typical of the new wave sweeping out what seemed to be to many of us the kitsch of the past. And, like generations of students before us, we thought rather smugly and egotistically that we had "found the way." However, regardless of what such high-handed rejection of the past would lead you to believe, it turns out that this choice was on firm ground after all. In truth, you can hardly beat white to set off the tempting colors of freshly prepared food.

Over the years more and more manufacturers joined the trend, giving us a tremendous number of whites to choose from in both bone china and rustic pottery.

The only hitch when you are combining white pieces from different sources is that they can be of either warm or cool tones—and often the two don't mix well, especially if they happen to fall at the far end of their respective spectrums. You might also encounter a similar problem when combining rustic with more refined china. The trick in both cases is to do the mixing with a purpose and not have it all jumbled in a haphazard way. For instance, a bowl of a very cool shade set on a warm or creamy-toned plate can look perfectly right, particularly if it is visually reinforced by being repeated around the table. Otherwise, you can hardly go wrong by choosing white.

Black, like white, can also be a wonderful foil for food. It is not as flexible, because, as good as it may be, it is still more limited by the number of food colors that look good against it. As an example, most salads, fruits, and vegetables are beautifully set off by black, but the same is not always true in the case of dark sauces, stews, and meats. This is not to say these foods actually look unappetizing, but rather that black doesn't make their color and texture "sing" as whites and some pastels might.

By pointing this out, I don't mean to suggest that you should agonize over this or even let it influence your choice too greatly. The bottom line is, if you like black, then you should have it. What I *am* saying is that by being aware of its limitations, you can compensate for them if you choose. One way would be to garnish dark meats with grated or stripped citrus rind or a lovely sprig of green placed on top of each portion. Or you might serve your stew in a small individual white (or other compatible color) bowl set on the plate.

Finally, I like black dinnerware not to have much of a sheen. Shiny black can look a bit too chic to me.

Now that I have had my say about the two extremes, let me add that there is an awful lot of fun in between, with plenty of shades and simple patterns that can be very appealing. I think that is amply illustrated on the previous pages and on the pages that follow. I genuinely like everything you see there. And I would not mind owning any of it. (As a matter of fact, I do own some of it.) But owning depends on budget—not to mention the storage space involved with having a large variety of china.

In my opinion, it is best to start with something basic that will serve almost all occasions and then add to it as your funds and space permit.

Over the years I have become increasingly fond of large plates—so much so that the old-fashioned standard size looks hopelessly underscaled to me. However, all sizes have their place. And, truthfully, plates have almost gotten too large of late—there is a point at which they become ungainly. (And, among other things, won't fit into the dishwasher.) My favorite size is eleven or eleven and a half inches. Certainly these are best for buffets.

But, like all other elements of your table service, this is a matter of personal taste. And I have been known to contradict my own "rules" on more than one occasion. How else can you account for the plate on page 75? Well, it just appealed to me—reason enough. So feel free!

SOURCES FOR FOLLOWING PAGES:
1. Christopher Idone "Millefiore" 12" porcelain dinner plate (additional pieces available) at Henri Bendel, 10 West 57th Street, New York, NY 10019.
2. Taitu for Lee Bailey 11" khaki porcelain dinner plate at Lee Bailey at Henri Bendel, 10 West 57th Street, New York, NY 10019.
3. Stainless steel 12¼" buffet plate by Bailey-Bannett Inc. at Lee Bailey at Henri Bendel, 10 West 57th Street, New York, NY 10019.
4. Taitu for Lee Bailey 11" gray porcelain dinner plate at Lee Bailey at Henri Bendel, 10 West 57th Street, New York, NY 10019.
5. Brown and ocher 11" spatterware dinner plate (additional pieces available) at Frank McIntosh at Henri Bendel, 10 West 57th Street, New York, NY 10019, and Frank McIntosh at Stanley Korshak, The Crescent, Dallas, TX 75201.
6. Silvestri 12" beechwood charger plate at Silvestri, 2720 North Paulina Street, Chicago, IL 60614, and at fine stores across the country.
7. Robert Haussmann for Swid Powell "Broken" 12" porcelain dinner plate (additional pieces available) at Sointu, 20 East 69th Street, New York, NY 10021.
8. White porcelain 10¼" dinner plate with thin gray band (additional pieces available) at D. F. Sanders, 386 West Broadway, New York, NY 10012, and 952 Madison Avenue, New York, NY 10021.
9. Gray Majolica-like 12" ceramic leaf plate (salad plate also available) at Frank McIntosh at Henri Bendel, 10 West 57th Street, New York, NY 10019, and Frank McIntosh at Stanley Korshak, The Crescent, Dallas, TX 75201.
10. White porcelain 10" dinner plate with thinly striped gray bands (additional pieces available) at Conran's Citicorp, 160 East 54th Street, New York, NY 10022.

1

2

5

8

Flatware

By a set of coincidental circumstances, I used the same flatware for almost all my life, from earliest childhood right up to a few years ago. The silver that my mother brought with her as a bride—which we always used, company or not—happened to be the same as my paternal grandmother's. And even as one of my aunts. So it was everywhere I went. I imagine that if I ever thought about such things, for a time I probably just assumed, with my child's logic, that all flatware was alike everyplace.

When it was time to set up my own first apartment, I had inherited my mother's silver. I would probably be using it even today if it had not been taken in a robbery. What I have now is David Mellor's "Pride" pattern, but I must admit that I am beginning to think maybe I should replace the original silver. It can still be ordered. This is not because I don't find the Mellor silver beautiful—I certainly do—or that there aren't numerous other patterns to choose from, many of which I actually like the design of better than my mother's. It is just that such a long indoctrination understandably imbued the original with more qualities to covet than mere pattern and weight.

It was also the sort of set that included everything imaginable, from iced tea spoons to fish forks to ice-cream forks. But it wasn't until after it was gone that I realized the convenience of having so much to choose from. Etiquette aside, having just the right fork or knife can make things work more smoothly. This message got through to me at a very early age. I remember complaining to my mother about being made to use a salad fork. Her response was to explain that eating salad was easier with its own fork because it has a sharper edge than a dinner fork, for cutting raw salad vegetables. And another time, how you don't need a great big soup spoon to eat cream soup with, as you would for daddy's favorite seafood gumbo. Or that the long handle of an iced tea spoon suits the tall iced tea glass. My silent acceptance of these little training sessions seems to have produced a complementary philosophical silence from her about the great clatter I could get out of this same tall glass when I was submitting it to the very vigorous stirring required to dissolve sugar and mix lemon juice into tea. She apparently appreciated that for young minds the heat of reason must be cooled by a little noisy action.

Obviously attitudes change over the years, and I have become, if anything, almost indifferent to such refinements, especially after getting a house in the country. Now I use anything that looks good and seems to work, even mixing it all up. Although my mother's logic still seems elegant.

When selecting flatware, the most important quality, after the basic look or design of it, is how it feels in the hand. This is one of the great faults I find with much of so-called modern flatware. From a design standpoint, it is often beautiful, but when picked up, its form doesn't caress the hand or fit it. There are patterns, for instance, with very thin round handles that feel to me as if I am trying to eat with pencils. Or those with wide, thin, flat handles—like eating with a couple of rulers. So I suppose if there is any subject on which I am traditional, it is flatware. The truth is, you probably can't undo those decades of holding the same knives and forks—which did feel good in the hand. Maybe this is the chicken-and-the-egg bit. What I grew up with feels right because I grew up with it.

But, good sport that I am, I have tried to be broad-minded here and have included things that I like the look of but am not as keen on the feel of as I might wish for. There is no use telling you which these are, because if it looks and feels good to you, it has passed the test.

There is also the consideration of whether you should buy silver, silver plate, or stainless steel. In the final analysis it seems to me that this would be decided by your budget (if you don't already have marriage silver) and how much time you are willing to spend keeping it bright. Good sterling requires polishing and also is a sizable investment. However, nothing looks and feels quite like it. This is for you to decide. Stainless requires hardly any care beyond wiping off a few water spots. I prefer the shiny finish myself because I like the way it looks as it begins to get used and scratched. Again, this is just a matter of personal taste.

I think salad forks are a good investment (not just because my mother explained them to me), because they can be used for pies and other desserts. The same with two sizes of soup spoons. But most of these choices will be dictated by the use you intend for them. How do you entertain? Maybe you don't like soup and never serve it. Maybe you do like iced tea and need long-handled spoons. Answer one question and it helps answer others.

Finally, does the household require more than one set of flatware—everyday and for company? My answer is, the only reason to have several sets is for variety, or if you have young children who might abuse it. Otherwise, you should put your best on the table every day. What is good improves with use and age.

SOURCES FOR FOLLOWING PAGES:
1. Chef Master plastic-handled flatware with nonstick Chefcoat at Lee Bailey at Henri Bendel, 10 West 57th Street, New York, NY 10019.
2. Gingo International "Chamonix" black-handled stainless steel flatware at Wolfman-Gold & Good Co., 484 Broome Street, New York, NY 10012, and 142 East 73rd Street, New York, NY 10021.
3. All matte-white Japanese flatware (also available in all black) at Lee Bailey at Henri Bendel, 10 West 57th Street, New York, NY 10019.
4. White porcelain pistol-handled stainless steel flatware at Wolfman-Gold & Good Co., 484 Broome Street, New York, NY 10012, and 142 East 73rd Street, New York, NY 10021.
5. Elsa Perreti "Padova" sterling silver flatware at Tiffany & Co., 727 Fifth Avenue, New York, NY 10022.
6. "Provence" ivory-colored plastic-handled stainless steel flatware at Wolfman-Gold & Good Co., 484 Broome Street, New York, NY 10012, and 142 East 73rd Street, New York, NY 10021.
7. Bistro ware stainless steel flatware at Wolfman-Gold & Good Co., 484 Broome Street, New York, NY 10012, and 142 East 73rd Street, New York, NY 10021.
8. David Mellor "Lotus" white-handled stainless steel flatware at Simon Pearce, 385 Bleecker Street, New York, NY 10014.
9. C'Ports "Aube" stainless steel flatware at D. F. Sanders, 386 West Broadway, New York, NY 10012, and 952 Madison Avenue, New York, NY 10021.
10. David Mellor "Provencal" black-handled with brass rivets stainless steel flatware at Simon Pearce, 385 Bleecker Street, New York, NY 10014.

Glassware

lthough I am a wine lover, I must admit that I do not consider myself to be a connoisseur by any stretch of the imagination (or ego). Maybe this has to do with all that iced tea I drank as a kid—and still love. Anyway, my wine drinking is mostly confined to meals in the evening, and then almost 90 percent of the time to red wine. That, at least in part, must account for my being so cavalier about what I serve wine in, for I'm perfectly happy with the all-purpose wineglasses. Or, in a pinch, a water glass. With or without a stem. I've never been one to be too much concerned with having the "right" glass for the right wine.

But, whichever glass you choose, it, like a dinner plate, should not compete with what it was designed to hold. My idea, then, of a perfect glass is one that seems to make the wine float in air and feels good in the hand.

The one exception to my "any good glass will do" approach is with champagne. I want champagne glasses to be the best, most graceful flutes. Luckily, there are many of these to choose from. Probably because I like the festivity champagne implies more than the actual wine itself, and since I seldom drink more than one glass, I want that glass to be a symbol of the specialness of the occasion the wine is meant to mark.

Fortunately, nowadays you can buy well-designed wineglasses in almost any price range, from those at the local department store all the way up to the supreme creations from the likes of Tiffany and Baccarat. So primarily your budget is your guide. That, and how important wine drinking is to you. Obviously, if you take your wine seriously you will likely be willing to spend a little more than if you can take it or leave it. And if you are in the latter category you certainly should not strain your budget. Funnily enough, though, I have found that people who like wine the least are almost equally as apt to indulge in expensive stemware as those who really do care.

For people who don't care about anything but the glass, I say "Mazel tov," but also I say be sure to get someone whom you can trust to advise you on the selection of wines. The best glass in the world can not do very much for a lousy wine. And, contrary to what some people are led to believe, good drinkable wine does not have to cost the earth. When selecting wines, we should be like those maddening French and understand the difference between a simple table wine and one fit for a grand meal and not confuse the two.

Within the boundaries of not competing with what the glass is meant to hold, there is a fair amount of leeway. Naturally, you want it to be in harmony with the plates you have selected—and I would suggest you select them first. So, for instance, if you have bought rustic pottery plates, no matter how pretty they are, a slim, thin-stemmed beauty from Baccarat will look a bit as if it is slumming next to them. My choice in such a case would be a heavy hand-blown style from Simon Pearce, or a reasonable approximation. On the other hand, if you are into refinement and have the budget, go for the Baccarat or Tiffany. It will be right at home and sure makes the wine sing.

The truth is that most of us fall into a category somewhere in the middle. I certainly do. There are times when refinement seems just swell and others when you don't want anything to do with it.

Although I know this probably runs counter to what a lot of people think is proper, it seems to me rather sad to own things that are "too good to use." If not now, when? Once the kids are past the stage of breaking everything in sight, why not treat yourself like a guest?

This brings to mind a very personal story I remember from when I was a young boy. My parents had a divorced friend who, with a teenage daughter, lived in genteel poverty with her mother. Their home was a crumbling but immaculate old plantation house, theirs to occupy courtesy of a cousin. It was filled with things from another, more privileged time. Among their heirlooms was a great quantity of silver, china, and crystal. Anyway, for reasons that are not important here, when I was about eleven years old—in the clear fading blue light of a still summer evening—I found myself there alone with the three of them, having dinner. The table was set in all its splendor. I might add, splendid in its quality and simplicity, not excess. I don't recall how it came up, but I remember the mother, who was quite old and proud, saying that they used their best every night, even when there was just family at dinner. As she explained: "It reminds us of what we are and that we must not allow ourselves to lose heart just because the Lord has decided that we must now live without money."

Well, that is a long way from selecting a glass to put wine in, but maybe not so far removed from how we should treat ourselves and our guests.

SOURCES FOR FOLLOWING PAGES:

Page 154, from left to right:
7¼" pilsner dessert glass at Conran's Citicorp, 160 East 54th Street, New York, NY 10022.
7¾" wineglass at Tiffany & Co., 727 Fifth Avenue, New York, NY 10022.
8⅞" pilsner/dessert glass at Dean & Deluca, 121 Prince Street, New York, NY 10012.
8¼" pilsner/dessert glass at Conran's Citicorp, 160 East 54th Street, New York, NY 10022.

Page 155, front row, from left to right:
6¾" Swid Powell cut glass goblet at Tiffany & Co., 727 Fifth Avenue, New York, NY 10022.
6" all-purpose wineglass at Dean & Deluca, 121 Prince Street, New York, NY 10012.
6½" French bistro wine/dessert glass at Lee Bailey at Henri Bendel, 10 West 57th Street, New York, NY 10019.
7½" classic wineglass at Dean & Deluca, 121 Prince Street, New York, NY 10012.

Page 155, back row and below, from left to right:
7" Baccarat all-purpose French wineglass at Tiffany & Co., 727 Fifth Avenue, New York, NY 10022.
7½" classic table wineglass at Dean & Deluca, 121 Prince Street, New York, NY 10012.
7¼" Christallerie Zwiesel all-purpose wineglass at Dean & Deluca, 121 Prince Street, New York, NY 10012.
7" classic all-purpose wineglass at Lee Bailey at Henri Bendel, 10 West 57th Street, New York, NY 10019.

Sources

COUNTRY HAM DINNER

Trend Pacific "Aspen" flatware and linen napkin, both at Frank McIntosh at Henri Bendel, 10 West 57th Street, New York, NY 10019, and Frank McIntosh at Stanley Korshak, The Crescent, Dallas, TX 75201.

10 oz. bar glass and Taitu 11″ dinner plate, both at Lee Bailey at Henri Bendel, 10 West 57th Street, New York, NY 10019; 7″ dessert glass at Conran's Citicorp, 160 East 54th Street, New York, NY 10022.

SUNNY SUMMER SALAD LUNCH

Yamazaki "Calibre" flatware at Neiman-Marcus stores across the country.

Tall glass tumbler at Williams-Sonoma, 576 Cutter Street, San Francisco, CA 94102, and Williams-Sonoma stores across the country.

Taitu for Tiffany 10½″ dinner plate (additional pieces available) at Tiffany & Co., 727 Fifth Avenue, New York, NY 10022.

Linen napkin at D. F. Sanders, 386 West Broadway, New York, NY 10012, and 952 Madison Avenue, New York, NY 10021.

OVEN FISH FRY

Christofle "Spatours" flatware, at Baccarat, 55 East 57th Street, New York, NY 10022.

Simon Pearce hand-blown Irish glass and linen napkin, both at Frank McIntosh at Henri Bendel, 10 West 57th Street, New York, NY 10019, and Frank McIntosh at Stanley Korshak, The Crescent, Dallas, TX 75201.

Limoges Claude Monet "Giverny" 11″ dinner plate (additional pieces available), at Tiffany & Co., 727 Fifth Avenue, New York, NY 10022; 24″ × 12″ ovenproof ceramic fish platter at Lee Bailey at Henri Bendel, 10 West 57th Street, New York, NY 10019.

SPECIAL SUMMER LUNCH

Georg Jensen "Michaelsen" flatware, at Royal Copenhagen, 683 Madison Avenue, New York, NY 10021.

Sven Jensen wineglass at Sointu, 20 East 69th Street, New York, NY 10021.

10½″ dinner plate at Pottery Barn, 117 East 59th Street, New York, NY 10022, and Bailey-Bannett Inc.; glass dessert bowl at Lee Bailey at Henri Bendel, 10 West 57th Street, New York, NY 10019.

Linen napkin at D. F. Sanders, 386 West Broadway, New York, NY 10012, and 952 Madison Avenue, New York, NY 10021.

GRILLED OUTDOOR SUPPER

Veralux French jelly glass at Williams-Sonoma, 576 Cutter Street, San Francisco, CA 94102, and Williams-Sonoma stores across the country.

Flatware at Wolfman Gold & Good Co., 484 Broome Street, New York, NY 10012, and 142 East 73rd Street, New York, NY 10021.

Linen napkin at Frank McIntosh at Henri Bendel, 10 West 57th Street, New York, NY 10019, and Frank McIntosh at Stanley Korshak, The Crescent, Dallas, TX 75201.

11¾″ buffet plate at Lee Bailey at Henri Bendel, 10 West 57th Street, New York, NY 10019.

OYSTER FRY

Taitu flatware, made in Japan, and Bailey-Bannett Inc. stainless steel dessert bowl and saucer, all at Lee Bailey at Henri Bendel, 10 West 57th Street, New York, NY 10019.

Beer stem glass at Williams-Sonoma, 576 Cutter Street, San Francisco, CA 94102, and Williams-Sonoma stores across the country.

Alsatian earthenware plate (additional pieces available), made in France, at Dean & Deluca, 121 Prince Street, New York, NY 10012.

Linen napkin at D. F. Sanders, 386 West Broadway, New York, NY 10012, and 952 Madison Avenue, New York, NY 10021.

Jade salt and pepper serving dish at Pine Street Antiques, Southampton, NY 11968.

CRAWFISH PASTA DINNER

Patino-Wolf "Nielo" flatware at Frank McIntosh at Henri Bendel, 10 West 57th Street, New York, NY 10019, and Frank McIntosh at Stanley Korshak, The Crescent, Dallas, TX 75201.

Tall glass tumbler (goblet available) at Wolfman-Gold & Good Co., 484 Broome Street, New York, NY 10012, and 142 East 73rd Street, New York, NY 10021.

Waldo Collection 10½″ dinner plate at Lee Bailey at Henri Bendel, 10 West 57th Street, New York, NY 10019.

Napkin at D. F. Sanders, 386 West Broadway, New York, NY 10012, and 952 Madison Avenue, New York, NY 10021.

THE LAST SUMMER LUNCH

C'Ports "Richelieu" flatware, made in France, at Dean & Deluca, 121 Prince Street, New York, NY 10012.

"Vins du Pays" 6″ wineglass at Pottery Barn, 117 East 59th Street, New York, NY 10022.

Bennington Potters 10½″ dinner plate at D. F. Sanders, 386 West Broadway, New York, NY 10012, and 952 Madison Avenue, New York, NY 10021; Bailey-Bannett Inc. glass bowl and stainless steel saucer at Lee Bailey at Henri Bendel, 10 West 57th Street, New York, NY 10019.

Linen napkin at Frank McIntosh at Henri Bendel, 10 West 57th Street, New York, NY 10019, and Frank McIntosh at Stanley Korshak, The Crescent, Dallas, TX 75201.

ELEGANT SATURDAY-NIGHT DINNER

David Mellor flatware, made in England, at Lee Bailey at Henri Bendel, 10 West 57th Street, New York, NY 10019.

6¼″ wineglass at Williams-Sonoma, 576 Cutter Street, San Francisco, CA 94102, and at Williams-Sonoma stores across the country.

Villeroy & Boch "Petite Fleur" 10½″ dinner plate (additional pieces available), at B. Altman & Co., 361 Fifth Avenue, New York, NY 10016.

Linen napkin at D. F. Sanders, 386 West Broadway, New York, NY 10012, and 952 Madison Avenue, New York, NY 10021.

WINTER SEAFOOD DINNER

Gray-handled flatware, 10½″ matte black dinner plate (additional pieces available), and linen napkin, all at D. F. Sanders, 386 West Broadway, New York, NY 10012, and 952 Madison Avenue, New York, NY 10021.

Progetti 5½″ wineglass at Pottery Barn, 117 East 59th Street, New York, NY 10022.

DINNER FOR A FROSTY EVENING

Christofle "Dupleix" flatware, made in France, and Limoges 11″ celadon dinner plate (additional pieces available), both at Baccarat, 55 East 57th Street, New York, NY 10022.

Richard Meier for Swid Powell wineglass at Frank McIntosh at Henri Bendel, 10 West 57th Street, New York, NY 10019, and Frank McIntosh at Stanley Korshak, The Crescent, Dallas, TX 75201.

Linen napkin at D. F. Sanders, 386 West Broadway, New York, NY 10012, and 952 Madison Avenue, New York, NY 10021.

FESTIVE BREAKFAST

Christofle "Chinon" flatware, made in France, and "George Sand" 9½" dinner plate (additional pieces available), both at Baccarat, 55 East 57th Street, New York, NY 10022.

8" goblet at Williams-Sonoma, 576 Cutter Street, San Francisco, CA 94102, and at Williams-Sonoma stores across the country.

Linen napkin at Frank McIntosh at Henri Bendel, 10 West 57th Street, New York, NY 10019, and Frank McIntosh at Stanley Korshak, The Crescent, Dallas, TX 75201.

MAKE-AHEAD DINNER

"President" flatware (2-piece serving set available), made in Italy, at Lee Bailey at Henri Bendel, 10 West 57th Street, New York, NY 10019.

7" wineglass at Dean & Deluca, 121 Prince Street, New York, NY 10012.

Rosenthal "Magic Flute" 11" dinner plate (other pieces available), at B. Altman & Co., 361 Fifth Avenue, New York, NY 10016.

Napkin at D. F. Sanders, 386 West Broadway, New York, NY 10012, and 952 Madison Avenue, New York, NY 10021.

SMALL BIRTHDAY PARTY

French bistro ware stainless steel flatware at Wolfman-Gold & Good Co., 484 Broome Street, New York, NY 10012, and 142 East 73rd Street, New York, NY 10021.

9¼" Wedgwood champagne flute at B. Altman & Co., 361 Fifth Avenue, New York, NY 10016.

Wineglass and Bailey-Bannett Inc. napkin both at Lee Bailey at Henri Bendel, 10 West 57th Street, New York, NY 10019.

VEGETABLE PASTA DINNER

Unmatched antique silverplate flatware and napkin, both at Wolfman-Gold & Good Co., 484 Broome Street, New York, NY 10012, and 142 East 73rd Street, New York, NY 10021.

10½" white-on-white dinner plate and saucer at Tiffany & Co., 727 Fifth Avenue, New York, NY 10022.

6" cut crystal goblet and Limoges "Hawthorne" 10¾" dinner plate (additional pieces available), both at Baccarat, 55 East 57th Street, New York, NY 10022.

SUMMER DINNER IN WINTER

Flatware at Conran's Citicorp, 160 East 54th Street, New York, NY 10022.

Kosta Boda 7¼" wineglass at Williams-Sonoma, 576 Cutter Street, San Francisco, CA 94102, and Williams-Sonoma stores across the country.

Coalport 10¾" dinner plate (additional pieces available) at Tiffany & Co., 727 Fifth Avenue, New York, NY 10022.

Napkin at Wolfman-Gold & Good Co., 484 Broome Street, New York, NY 10012, and 143 East 73rd Street, New York, NY 10021.

LUNCH FOR A COLD SUNDAY AFTERNOON

"Baquette" flatware, made in France, at Lee Bailey at Henri Bendel, 10 West 57th Street, New York, NY 10019.

Val St. Lambert 7¼" wineglass at Dean & Deluca, 121 Prince Street, New York, NY 10012.

"Famille Verte" 10½" dinner plate (additional pieces available), reproduced by and available at the Metropolitan Museum of Art, Fifth Avenue and 82nd Street, New York, NY 10028.

Linen napkin at Frank McIntosh at Henri Bendel, 10 West 57th Street, New York, NY 10019, and Frank McIntosh at Stanley Korshak, The Crescent, Dallas, TX 75201.

WINTER CHICKEN DINNER

David Mellor "Java" flatware and linen napkin, both at D. F. Sanders, 386 West Broadway, New York, NY 10012, and 952 Madison Avenue, New York, NY 10021.

Simon Pearce goblet and Gwathmey Siegel for Swid Powell "Tuxedo" 12" dinner plate (additional pieces available), both at Frank McIntosh at Henri Bendel, 10 West 57th Street, New York, NY 10019, and Frank McIntosh at Stanley Korshak, The Crescent, Dallas, TX 75201.

FALL SUNDAY LUNCH

Nicolas Johns flatware, made in England, and all-purpose bistro glass, both at Lee Bailey at Henri Bendel, 10 West 57th Street, New York, NY 10019.

Bennington Potters 10½" dinner plate (additional pieces available) at D. F. Sanders, 386 West Broadway, New York, NY 10012, and 952 Madison Avenue, New York, NY 10021.

Linen napkin at Frank McIntosh at Henri Bendel, 10 West 57th Street, New York, NY 10019, and Frank McIntosh at Stanley Korshak, The Crescent, Dallas, TX 75201.

EASY FISH DINNER

"Alta" European flatware, stainless steel salt and pepper shakers, heavy stem glass goblet, and linen napkin, all at Frank McIntosh at Henri Bendel, 10 West 57th Street, New York, NY 10019, and Frank McIntosh at Stanley Korshak, The Crescent, Dallas, TX 75201.

10¾" dinner plate (additional pieces available) at Sointu, 20 East 69th Street, New York, NY 10021.

MY BEST PORK ROAST DINNER

French stainless steel flatware at Wolfman-Gold & Good Co., 484 Broome Street, New York, NY 10012, and 142 East 73rd Street, New York, NY 10021.

8" all-purpose wineglass at D. F. Sanders, 386 West Broadway, New York, NY 10012, and 952 Madison Avenue, New York, NY 10021.

Wedgwood 11" drabware dinner plate (additional pieces available) at Tiffany & Co., 727 Fifth Avenue, New York, NY 10022.

Linen napkin at Frank McIntosh at Henri Bendel, 10 West 57th Street, New York, NY 10019, and Frank McIntosh at Stanley Korshak, The Crescent, Dallas, TX 75201.

Antique silver salt and pepper shakers at Pine Street Antiques, Southampton, NY 11968.

Index